THE TWO OF US

Larry J. Uhrig

The Two of Us

Affirming, Celebrating and Symbolizing Gay and Lesbian Relationships

Boston: Alyson Publications, Inc.

Acknowledgments

Special thanks and appreciation must be given to the following persons without whose help and guiding influence this book could never have been written:

Dick and Diane Morrison for giving me living symbols of love and relationship when all my other symbols were crumbling around me.

Don Mauck and Ed Meyer for teaching me the practice and power of communicating and for their patience, love and faith.

Jim and Steve for giving me Hawaii as a place of rest and writing, to Jack and Nick for giving me Maui, and to my dear Kevin for Maui and much more.

Bob for vision and prophecy, Eric for endless hospitality, to the "children" for being the "children."

Beth and Dana for hard work, belief in the book, editorial skills, wisdom and yet another model.

Deacon and Jim for inspiration and commitment to making this book happen and for allowing me to share in the blessing of their relationship.

And certainly not least, perhaps first: Troy D. Perry for changing the world and being a faithful friend.

This is a paperback original from Alyson Publications, Inc., PO Box 2783, Boston, MA 02208. Distributed in England by Gay Men's Press, PO Box 247, London, N15 6RW.

First edition, December 1984   5 4 3 2 1

ISBN 0 932870 62 7

Contents

To Alan
who embodies the reality of these words

To my mother
a saint of God, who teaches the meaning of love

To gay men and women everywhere
your dreams shall come true

To the members and friends of the
Metropolitan Community Church of Washington, DC
a place of healing, vision, and life
for me and thousands of gay people

Preface

by The Rev. Troy D. Perry, Founder
Universal Fellowship of
Metropolitan Community Churches

The final issue of *Life* magazine, in 1972, carried the story of the founding of Metropolitan Community Church in Los Angeles. Of all the photographs shown in this article, the one showing two men being "married" in the church drew the most attention. Both in the gay and non-gay communities, people wrote me, literally from all over the world, with letters full of reactions ranging from shock to curiosity to real questions about relationships within the gay and lesbian community.

Twelve years later the press shows the same interest in what we, with the Universal Fellowship of Metropolitan Community Churches, call "Holy Union." This year, reporters from *People* magazine, while doing a story on Metropolitan Community Church, received permission to photograph a service of Holy Union. I learned the curiosity is still there. At long last, someone has taken the time to write a comprehensive book to explain why more and more gay and lesbian couples are turning to the church for these Rites of Blessing and what happens at them, as well as explaining what makes for a good relationship.

You have in your hands the finest book on gay relationships that I have had the pleasure of reading. Larry J. Uhrig, the author of *The Two of Us*, is a long-time member of the Universal Fellowship of Metropolitan Community Churches and is pastor of one of our most successful congregations, Metropolitan Community Church in Washington, DC. Larry has had vast experiences in not only the role of pastor, but also as counselor. In writing *The Two of Us*, he has drawn on his long experience in counseling to talk about the real nitty-gritty of building a relationship.

One of my favorite parts of the book is a series of nine true life stories about how couples have *unsuccessfully* responded to the issue of relationships, which is intended to indicate the pitfalls we so easily fall into and to share some of the rather absurd realities which occur. Following that section of the book is the real meat of the text. Larry, as a Christian minister, addresses the nature of spirituality and sexuality and the task of gay persons to unite these two factions of life into a productive whole.

The theological and Biblical symbols of our culture are addressed in a way that reforms them and defines the nature of blessing. The implications of this section seriously challenge the traditions of the Western Church and seek to offer substantial hope to all people interested in symbolizing the bonding process.

I cannot recommend this book enough. It is must reading for all gay men and lesbians looking for that "special person" to include in their lives, as well as couples that are already in their life's journey with each other. This book should also be read by heterosexuals who are interested in knowing more about their gay neighbors.

The Rev. Troy D. Perry
Universal Fellowship of Metropolitan Community Churches
5300 Santa Monica Blvd.
Los Angeles, CA 90029

Foreword

I had to write this book. I had to have a way to express all the things I have been seeing and feeling. Two factors produce my response in writing: they are frustration and hope.

First frustration. I guess I would use a stronger word like anger, but I will stay with frustration. Years of counseling with gay couples and of watching individuals attempting to form a relationship have produced a deep and unsettling frustration within me. I have watched myself and others chase after the myth of the knight in shining armor. Men and women alike have longed for the return of the Greek gods and goddesses that we might lie with them as did the heroes and heroines of the Greek tragedy we were raised on. We have longed to run off to a little white picket fence in the country or some similar secluded place. All of this has suggested to us that having a relationship that lasted was the result of some serendipitous cupid whose arrow eventually found our heart. In frustration we have fled lover after lover, spouse after spouse.

Watching these scenarios leaves me ready to shout to the world, "Wait. Stop. It doesn't have to be that way. There is hope!"

Hope is found in knowing that two persons can have a relationship if they truly want one. Hope is knowing couples who have been together for many, many years. Hope is knowing that the stereotypical statement, "Gay relationships don't last" is a lie perpetuated by ignorance. Hope is found in the practice of living, *one day at a time*. It is found in learning to communicate, in discovering honesty and trust. Hope comes from the deep self-awareness that I will never meet all the needs of another person and that they will never meet all of my needs. This wonderful awareness certainly sets one free to accept the other person for who they are and who they are not.

So I sat down one day and started writing. The wonder of the task was that all these words just started flowing out of me like a dam had broken. I hope that this flood will water previously barren places in the lives of gay and lesbian people. I hope for growth in our self-awareness and self-esteem, for strength in our relationships and in our confidence about tomorrow. And so this flood of words has become a hopeful gift born out of frustration and no small amount of anger and pain. The joy for me is in knowing that after pain comes healing, and with healing there is both growth and wisdom. As gay men and women, we are on the brink of a new future — a future which will see our self-integration, our discovery of power and gifts from within. That which we will discover will not be things others shall give us, but rather gifts and graces, powers and talents already latent in our bones. This fire in our bones will be let out for the world to see its brightness and its glory, a light to chart the future by, a warmth to keep us together and in peace through all dark, cold, and stormy nights.

My deeper hope is that this book will be a part of the prelude to our decade of destiny, the 1990s; that it will be a piece of the foundation of each of our futures; that it will be both fresh air and healing tonic to the oppressions of the past; and, yes, that it will even be a battle cry for us to assault the symbols of our times with the gifts and reality of ourselves.

We have a reason to affirm who we are. We have a reason to celebrate this affirmation, and it is time to symbolize our meaning for the generations which shall come after us, our spiritual children whose freedom is assured in our coming out to liberty.

Larry J. Uhrig
Washington, DC
January 1984

1

What do you mean, "We want to get married"?

"We want to get married. Will you marry us?" That is the essence of the question being posed almost daily by gay and lesbian couples to clergy ministering to the gay community in this country.

The phone rings at all hours of the day and night with these plaintive requests for someone, somehow, to formalize their civilly unsanctioned relationships. And yet, among these couples there is scarcely a common denominator: some have been together for a week, some a month or several months and others for years; some even call fresh from a night on the town with the newly discovered love of their life.

Though they expect nothing more than a simple yes or no from the call, it is clear that each caller is looking for some legal sanction to a gay relationship, only to discover or to have confirmed that legalization of same-sex relationships does not exist in the United States.

What else are they looking for? What do they want? In my experience they are looking for four things, perhaps in varying degrees: (1) affirmation of the relationship; (2) celebration of the relationship; (3) symbolization of the relationship; and (4) something beyond tradition.

The Need for Affirmation

In every relationship — in every coupling of adult individuals — there is some quest for social sanction and affirmation of the bonding. Persons in relationships need others who play significant roles in their lives to affirm the union. This need is met in several ways in our culture. In traditional heterosexual culture, there is the sometimes ominous but always important event of introducing one's espoused to one's family. This may even be a somewhat formal event with painstaking detail given to circumstance and setting. The desired result is, of course, the family's affirmation of the couple, acceptance of the spouse, and an endorsement of the relationship.

The less formal "presentation" of the relationship occurs as, over time, the spouse is introduced to friends and co-workers. Here, again, the experience is designed to elicit approval and acknowledgment from peers and family with the expectation, whether realized or not, that these people will offer nurture, encouragement and support as the relationship develops.

Since this is the social norm in our culture, homosexual couples clearly encounter a sizable barrier even at the outset. Except for those who are out to the world, few of us can safely introduce our love or spouse to our co-workers, or even to all our friends; family introductions also pose special problems. Our inability, unlike our brothers and sisters in the heterosexual world, to shout our love from the rooftops or even quietly to whisper it in our workplaces or at family reunions deprives us of complete social acceptance and affirmation of our relationships. The search for affirmation thus not unexpectedly leads gay and lesbian couples often to seek some social equivalent of the traditional marriage rite.

It is important to distinguish between the religious, spiritual and social function of marriage and the entirely separate legal function of marriage. Tradition in the United States has delegated the function of representing the state's interests in legalizing relationships between men and women to the church. While secular justices of the peace have always been available for this purpose, the usual method of solemnizing marriage has been through the clergy. It is not unusual even for those who profess no particular faith to rely on the church to formalize their marriage, merely to conform to societal norms. The "necessary" compromise of faith weakens the religious institution of marriage as it becomes co-opted by the needs of the state. It further confuses the affirmation of the couple with the legal transaction of marriage.

It is perhaps time for us in the United States to adopt the European method whereby all couples seeking marriage use a two-step process of legalizing their "contract" of marriage under sanction of the state and then, if they are persons of faith, pursue a religious blessing of the "spiritual contract" in their selected church or synagogue. Unfortunately, that process seems unlikely to gain much immediate favor in the United States as we cling to what is expected of us. We may, therefore, be bound to continue to live with ambiguity as to the meaning of marriage, with the legal, moral, ethical, social and spiritual components of the rite being intertwined and indistinct pieces of the marriage contract.

The Need for Celebration

Every couple that has made some sort of mutual commitment and received a degree of social affirmation of this covenant usually seeks a celebration of this wonderful process.

The social demands of tradition usually prescribe some form of "wedding" as the celebration. Unfortunately, more time is devoted often to the style of the wedding than to more fundamental questions such as preparedness, maturity, counseling and self-examination, or to such critical issues as co-habitation, sex, financial management, conflict resolution, or even the handling of simple everyday habits of two separate individuals. Some of these questions may crop up along the path to the wedding but typically they are considered secondary to more "pressing" issues such as the size of the wedding party, the guest list, the identity of the best man or maid of honor, and other questions devolving from the socio-economic statement that the couple (or their well-intentioned parents) strive to make.

For gay couples, the approaches to a celebration of union are different. The usual social customs are not addressed to us. It is obvious from the outset that this custom and stimulus for celebration does not fit the reality of gay and lesbian couples. For most, there are no readily available ways to celebrate their love and commitment. It is time for us to create symbols that are new and appropriate, while at the same time serving the function of traditional symbols.

The Needs for Symbolization

Coalescing with the need for affirmation and celebration is a more basic need which I call "symbolization." Deep within each individual who becomes coupled in a loving relationship is the need to symbolize in outward and physical form the inner spiritual, emotional, and psychological experience of the union. This need is met traditionally by the marriage ceremony and, more specifically, by the ceremony's vows, blessing, the witness of friends and family, the exchange of rings and the neatly inscribed certificate from the county clerk.

Every culture throughout human history has had some form of outward sign to acknowledge, even advertise, the union of two persons. However, until recently gay and lesbian couples were exempt from this history and were left without benefit of any of the socially acknowledged symbols. With both church and state working in concert to define the rites and symbols of relationships, there has been little for us to do except perhaps to convene a party among friends to make some sort of public statement or perhaps to privately exchange vows with one another alone or with a handful of accepting friends. Many couples have come to me to describe their private vows, perhaps made standing upon a beach or a mountaintop, expressing their love and commitment to each other. And yet, they come looking for something more. Now, that something more is available.

Breaking Away from the Traditional Socialization

Whether a couple consists of two men, two women, or a man and a woman, all couples want to affirm, symbolize and celebrate their relationship. The scale of this activity may vary greatly, but these needs are always present.

What is essential for gay couples, and is desirable for "traditional" couples, is a new understanding of marriage — a new approach to meeting these three needs. This new approach must begin, I believe, by separating the social, psychological and spiritual aspects of a relationship from its legal recognition. Unquestionably, the legal recognition of a relationship has its place; such questions as inheritance, property ownership, taxation, and definition of the rights of children require a clear legal relationship between the two individuals. However, even without the legal sanction of the state, it is possible for lesbian and gay couples to resolve many of these issues and achieve most of the same ends as a legal marriage through carefully drawn legal instruments.

All couples should examine these several perspectives of a relationship separately: (1) the legal questions, (2) social sanction of the relationship, and (3) fulfillment of the three basic needs discussed above (affirmation, celebration and symbolization).

Gay men and women free themselves from the social straitjackets of tradition in order to explore and discover that, indeed, they are capable of finding affirmation, celebration and symbolization of their relationships without compromising their personal integrity. While traditional forms for the expression of love between two people have been useful in the past and may be useful in the present for men and women in heterosexual relationships, we as gay people must understand that our desired goals are not dependent upon traditional forms.

A tragedy of our society may be the natural but unfitting attempt of two men or two women trying to fit themselves into the model of their parents' relationships. When gay people seek to copy heterosexual marriage, the result is almost certainly a severe compromise of selfhood and subjugation to symbol and form which often contains an implied denunciation of one's identity.

The response to the question "Will you marry us?" must be a careful and exciting exploration of what a couple is really asking for. Why do you want this ceremony? What do you want it to achieve? How can it express who you are — your history and expressions of love?

To respond to these questions requires closely examining a relationship, the scope of the mutual com-

mitment, and the context in which the union will be
lived out. How will the couple relate to family, work
and friends? What is the spiritual and religious expression of the relationship and how does the lack of
social sanction affect life together? Are you "out of the
closet" — both of you or just one? What do your families know of your lifestyle?

This may seem like an endless and probing stream
of personal and intimate questions, but it is an essential foundation upon which the histories of two people can truly be affirmed, really celebrated, and honestly symbolized.

The "bottom line" is that a couple can seek to
commemorate their relationship in virtually any
manner they choose as long as both are honest with
each other and are committed to work at the relationship one day at a time. A gay couple can discover the
real essence of covenant in the old marriage form and
bring to this essence the reality and truth of their
lives. In the end, this is a joyful task which lends hope
and stability to all our relationships. In the chapters
ahead, we will explore both the myths and major pitfalls which often stand in the way of stable, long-
lasting gay relationships. We will look at the learning
of relationship skills, tools for successful living together and, in closing, look at some profound spiritual, historical, and theological realities as gay people
become the prophetic vehicle for the essential union
of spirituality and sexuality.

2
Demystifying
the romantic myth

Hollywood's Curse

It may be inherently unfair to blame the movie industry for what I am about to describe, but it represents a convenient scapegoat easily understood by most of us. You see, this "curse" actually started long before talking pictures, as the literature of romance filled our minds with images of love so powerful it was capable of altering the course of nations.

Romance is indeed wonderful; I am the last to deny its force or its ability to transform lives and nations. But I believe we need to examine both romance and passion in the context of reality without, at the same time, diminishing their power.

The larger-than-life romance of the silver screen has caused many of us to discount our own romantic encounters. We have measured our experience by the standards of others, no matter how fanciful or unrealistic; into our model of romantic love we have incorporated measures and standards that no mortal will ever be able to achieve.

We are entranced with myths such as "there is one Mr. Wonderful" or "one Ms. Right" somewhere in the universe waiting for us. Innocently, we thereby set up a "needle in the haystack" scenario with monumental odds against finding our one perfectly matched mate. We have thus started our quest for love on a negative footing with low expectations of success.

Just as we are enthralled with the "true love" that our movie heroes and heroines seem to find without effort, we also expect the typically painful termination of the romance as fictional lovers end their experience with an epithet such as "I'm sorry it didn't work out between us." Just what is the "it" that didn't work out? This approach suggests that there is some objective state of blissful existence called love that we magically enter, or more commonly fall into — and some arbitrary goddess of love whimsically choosing who will be endowed with "it." And what does "work out" mean? The fatalistic phrase "it just didn't work out" suggests that we are innocent and passive bystanders who have utterly no control over our experiences. But we are not.

All too often we have allowed the glamour of Hollywood romance to rob us of the wonders of real love in our own lives. Without the elaborate movie sets, without the skillful makeup artist's touch and the costumer's elegant fittings, our own love may seem mundane indeed. Vested with only ordinary looks, mortal shortcomings, and — heaven forbid — perhaps even blemishes and paunches around the middle, our own lover will inevitably fall short of the Hollywood myth. This strikes at the very heart of much of our romantic societal dysfunction. We are willing to accept that others may have had great lovers but our own low self-esteem renders us unable to accept such magnificent love for ourselves. We just don't think of ourselves as lovable. Who would, after all, really love me? The trap lurking in every successful relationship is right here. If we cannot love and accept ourselves as we are, then we may as well abandon all hope that another will love and accept us. The secret of finding love is loving yourself.

Shopping List Lovers — Seduced by the Marketplace

Because of the Hollywood romantic myth, our culture is saturated with false images of what is desirable in a lover. This confronts us at every turn, as we look for the consummate lover with a host of *ideal* traits.

The market image of the desirable lover has a heavy accent on youth, beauty, property, education, and, of course, exceptional sexual prowess. Exemplary of the latter is the virtual obsession with one's relative size; unless one is sexually endowed, one might as well forget the possibility of attaining a successful relationship. We may even feel guilty and inadequate because we feel we do not meet the social measures of sexual attractiveness.

Many of us are driven by a perpetual shopping spree for the "right lover." We have mentally concocted a special shopping list of what we want. Visualize it — it is like going to the supermarket with a list of the traits and characteristics we wish and need for our own emotional nurture. We walk through the routine of life either consciously or unconsciously checking those we meet against our list. Our list includes a certain range of ages, a desired profession or a list of "acceptable" ones, a minimal salary range, a certain level of educational attainment, and a given family background or religious affiliation. The list is also engraved with our own minimum qualifications as to physique and sexual repertoire.

I am not intimating that it is wrong to have concocted such a list. What I am saying is this: upon careful examination, we would undoubtedly find that much of our list was not even dictated by our own needs, but was prescribed instead by friends, family, custom, social vogue or even Hollywood myth.

More important, when we meet another person we are probably so preoccupied with checking that person against the characteristics on the list that we fail to see that he or she possesses traits that are even more desirable. We don't allow the person to demonstrate his or her true nature and real qualities. We often foreclose the possibility of any further relationship with people merely because they failed to meet one of our crucial criteria.

Now complicate this already impossible scenario with the likelihood that two persons are both out "shopping" in this manner. The odds of the two meeting, exploring one another, and developing a relationship are incredibly small.

It is important for each of us to realize that we are operating with a *de facto* list and then to carefully examine those characteristics we have so inflexibly determined are essential for our ideal lover. Where did we derive the criteria? This kind of examination may well convince us that we have no idea how our list was formed.

I suspect we all harbor some form of composite image of whom we might select as our life's partner, only to discover that the person with whom we eventually couple doesn't look one iota like that image. Unfortunately, the shopping list *problem* does not vanish with the onset of a mature relationship. It is often difficult to escape the constant seduction of the marketplace, where there is a persistent outside pressure on any relationship to define it and manage its expression. This factor affects all couples.

Cohabitation and Compatibility

The real test of a relationship begins with moving in together. Dating over a period of weeks or months may be the typical beginning for any relationship but the courting period gives us a glimpse only of the surface of another person. And, in the early glow of the relationship, that surface is made up of the images that we consciously select to be seen. We can all recall those first dates when, with decided lack of intellectual honesty, we slanted our avowed likes and dislikes to what we thought would be most appreciated by our date. In the early dating stages, the superficial glimpse of our date may consist not only of a number of intentionally false signals but of the most obvious traits of the person: their family background, job, education, socio-economic status, menu choices, movie selections, dance steps and, if the relationship is truly geared to discussion, the religious background of the person. The real nitty-gritty of a relationship comes only with cohabitation.

I maintain, both from observation of hundreds of couples and from experience, that you never really know another person until you live with them — sharing a bathroom and all of the other mundane tasks of everyday life. Living together for a year or more is really only the beginning point of knowing one another. A friend of mine says that the true test of whether you have opened the door to getting to know someone is whether you feel free to exhibit unavoidable flatulence in their presence. Only then can you be sure the person feels free to be himself or herself around you.

Of course, cohabitation is also a time of marvelous discovery of each other. It is the opportunity to deepen and test what was begun or maybe only hinted at during the courting stage.

The decision to move in together should be preceded by serious discussion of each individual's wants, needs, goals, and lifestyle. The more two people can openly talk about all of the details and dynamics of their prospective life together, the more likely they are to achieve a successful relationship.

In the early stages, when two people are making that difficult and sometimes frightening decision to combine their separate households, it is important to look seriously at several levels of compatibility. Each couple will have their own special niches of compatibility to explore, but there are some common factors that any two people should examine before moving in together. These include age, education, socioeconomic status, lifestyle, religion and sex. The more divergent the positions of the two on each of these issues, the greater the possibility of ultimate conflict and the lower the likelihood that a successful relationship will result. Let us look at each of these areas briefly.

Age

While generalizations are difficult, the potential for difficulty in communication and compatibility heightens as the age difference between the two partners increases. Among differing generations, divergent worldviews and lifestyles are inevitable.

A number of gay men I have known in the later stages of middle age have universally selected young men in their late adolescent development as prospective partners and then have pondered why the relationship did not succeed. While a significant difference in age (or in any other key factor) may not alone doom a relationship, the more areas of divergence, the greater the compatibility problem the couple can expect to encounter.

Education

Again, the rule seems to be that the greater the difference in educational accomplishments, the greater the potential for discord. I will continue to deal here with the extremes in order to emphasize a point; however, even subtle differences may, over time, erode an otherwise successful relationship. If one person with a graduate degree enters into a relationship with a high school drop-out, the two are likely to have some substantial differences in their worldviews. Many of the problems in this area will center upon how individuals interpret and express the meaning of their life experiences, and more particularly, their mutually shared life experience. The range of difference in this area is also likely to trigger a substantial difference in income.

Socio-Economic Status

This is, of course, an almost limitless category encompassing a host of other factors. If the income level of an individual is, for example, in excess of $50,000 a year and the other survives on the minimum wage, the problems are obvious. How will they mutually determine their living standard as a couple? Will there be difficulties on the key questions of independence and self-respect? The person at the low end of the range may suffer from the denigrating concept of being *kept* as a result of financial dependence on the other.

Lifestyles

This category may be thought as of a function of all the other factors, but it is also important as a separate area. When two individuals decide to live together, yet differ widely on such fundamental lifestyles issues as what constitutes acceptable relaxation, what represents the optimum vacation, what social patterns are to be adopted, how finances are to managed, and the like, then distinct problems lie ahead.

Religion

The question of religion is often scarcely mentioned in the early stages of a relationship, except perhaps in passing as one recounts for the first time one's personal history. Religion is often regarded as a personal matter with little bearing on the ultimate success of a relationship. How misguided is this notion! The truth is that religion and faith lie at the core of the symbols used to interpret life, ascribe value, and define meaning. It is dangerous to shy away from an early exploration of this subject.

If one of you has strong religious convictions and the other has none, you are again confronted with the material for discord. Often, one or both persons had strong or even rigid religious training as a youth but has abandoned it as an adult. Since the religion is not being "practiced," you may deem it to play but a minor part in life's scheme. At the same time, both of you may be defining and evaluating your relationship — indeed your lives — in terms of the religious symbols you acquired in childhood without realizing that you are doing so.

This is a common problem among gay couples; many of us have shied away from a religion which condemns our sexuality. Thus, we may not consider ourselves particularly religious, while actually we are operating from a base of strong religious traditions. This ambiguity about religion accounts for much of today's relationship counseling and therapy. Frequently, the religious roots of conflict and guilt in a relationship are not evident upon superficial examination and are discovered only after a crisis in the relationship has occurred and there has been a deep probing of the cause of the crisis.

Sex

While the influence of religion is often ignored, the discussion of sexual differences is often unduly emphasized. It is certain that sex need not be the defining factor in any relationship. Nevertheless, we must at least acknowledge that wide differences in the levels of sexual desire, forms of expression, sharing of fantasy, and the fulfillment of needs can hurt a relationship. No two persons will have precisely the same level of sexual needs, no matter how apparently compatible. Similarly, no one person will be able to meet every need of the other partner at all times.

How the two of you elect to resolve your real sexual differences is important. It will affect how you reduce tension, anxiety, frustration, and hostility. In resolving this conflict you must also maintain the dignity and self-worth of each of you. This is the failing point of those relationships whose success is determined on the basis of sex, as one or both partners engage in games using sex as a weapon or for barter. In this issue, a wide range of divergence must be caringly addressed, and you may want the assistance of a professional counselor or pastor.

Other factors could be added to this compatibility list; the several key items discussed above are by no means comprehensive. But the real point here is to point out that there are areas in which substantial differences are built-in invitations for conflict. When differences are encountered in more than one key area, the relationship, while not doomed to failure, poses a special challenge to the participants.

Fortunately, working through these differences can be a rewarding task in itself. Given a mutual intent to "make it work," you can sit down and talk through many of the differences you may encounter. Still further differences will no doubt appear as you continue to live together. That is all the more reason to live together for a substantial period of time before formalizing or celebrating your relationship. That will allow for the slow and careful discovery — and resolution — of further differences which may, if allowed to go unnoticed, be serious.

3

Falling in love

A colleague of mine, the Rev. Don Eastman in Dallas, Texas, received a phone call from a young man he had been counseling. The caller was ecstatically happy that he had met the man of his dreams, and was "madly in love." He asked if Don would perform a Holy Union for him and his lover. Don's response was, "I am very happy for you. How long have you known your friend?" The reply: "Three days." Don's response was: "It's not love you're in, it's heat."

A woman called me one day to tell me of her new lover and to inquire if I were available to "marry" them on Saturday because her lover was in the Army and had to return to Europe for three years. They "just had to get married!"

These two accounts show vividly the levels of confusion among many people: confusion about what love is on the one hand and how to express it on the other.

We often mistake strong biological urges for love; we mistake the reception of an affectionate response for love; and we even mistake the words "I love you," however innocently spoken, for the real human experience of love. Certainly two people are capable, even at first meeting, of enjoying an immediate attraction, sensitivity, and bonding. Yet it is my firm conviction that love is a learning, growing experience resulting from time, trust, and mutual giving. To love a person means to accept them just as they are. It means allowing them to be everything they are and even what they are not. Love is freedom and permission to be. It is this freedom and permission that enables growth and change. In this context, two people can grow toward one another and become united in a bonding which lasts.

You cannot know if you love another person until and unless you have spent time together, have communicated honestly and deeply, and have lived together. You may like, appreciate, and love certain qualities, ideologies, behavior, or personality traits; but these do not, even in the aggregate, equal love. Love must be the product of mutual exploration and examination over a period of time. This time is measured in years, not weeks. Love is an ongoing process of discovery and disclosure requiring both honesty and trust. Without these qualities, love has very little chance to survive — it becomes like a withering plant without water.

In our daily lives we encounter so many myths, assumptions and social stereotypes about love and romance that it is hard to identify even the presence of love. So many emotions are mistaken for love that commitments are made again and again on no more stable a foundation than a high degree of body temperature.

The social ethic of American culture stresses being coupled and bonded so strongly that young men and women have, as a matter of obedience and fulfillment of expectation, blindly entered into marriage — often with no thought or examination. They unite their lives with one another. They encumber their lives with legal contracts, children and all the trappings of marriage. Years later, they discover unhappiness and alienation that could have been avoided.

The sorrow and tragedy is evident in watching two adults discover that they joined together only because it was expected of them; it was what everyone else was doing. Later, they discovered not only that their marriage was a sham but that they did not even love each other.

This is a social pattern that both heterosexual and gay couples must avoid. Often, a gay man or lesbian will follow this pattern of heterosexual marriage only to discover they are living a lie — a lie which is painfully difficult to recognize, or to share with their partner. For the sake of family, children, and friends, the lie may frequently be perpetuated into an utter lifetime of misery.

Time is On Your Side

"But do you love me?" is a question that can be truthfully answered only with time.

Time is one of the most precious gifts to any relationship: time to discover, time to express, time to live — this is the gift every person must come to embrace if he or she wishes to build a life in union with another.

Taking time can best be illustrated by an analogy. The death of a loved one is not unlike the break-up of a relationship. A person goes through the same stages of grieving: denial, anger, depression, and acceptance, which may seem to take an eternity. In fact, the process of living through these stages may take a year or longer, even into a subsequent relationship. The experience of loss — loss of expectations, loss of one's personal identity — takes time to work through. You must understand the process and the time needed to grieve to be equipped to face the pain and anger which follow.

A serious problem occurs if residual anger from a prior relationship gets vented on the new partner. If the source of this anger is not identified, the new spouse will take it personally. What can result is conflict and even separation. An understanding of what we are feeling, and why, is essential for us to process residual anger.

Since the grieving process can last for an extended period of time, a couple must allow time to pass so that the anger can be purged without tainting the new relationship.

My own experience confirms this. I discovered only after many months with my spouse that I was responding to him with anger and hurt which were really directed at my first lover. Without realizing it, I would react with anger and push my spouse away emotionally for little reason. Only through his sensitivity and compassion did I discover unresolved conflict and anger never before expressed. To my amazement, it took almost three years to apprehend fully that my behavior was related to my first relationship. I have thus come to believe the following rule: an extended relationship which suffers from a break-up will have residual effects upon subsequent relationships and will, in turn, require a period of healing and understanding. In my case, three years were required to conclude the grieving and healing process. The spouse of a person going through grief from the loss of a former partner must understand these dynamics and patiently grant the necessary time to conclude the grief process.

The grief process must and will ultimately complete itself. Attempting to avoid this process will only add stress and conflict. Such avoidance, if prolonged, may seriously jeopardize the health of your current relationship. The grieving and healing process may extend from former relationships into current ones, thus complicating the dynamics of the relationship. The circumstances under which a prior relationship ended may affect the new relationship.

I recently counseled two women contemplating a Holy Union. One, a bright and intense person, had lost her husband through suicide. He had said, "If you leave me, I'll kill myself." But she knew she could no longer endure the relationship. She walked out the door, only to hear the sound of a gunshot as he fulfilled what she hoped had been only an idle threat. For twelve years, she carried a sense of guilt and responsibility for his death. This event is still a prominent factor in her life as she seeks to build a relationship with a woman who clearly loves and supports her. The dramatic, violent and painful ending of her marriage continues to persist as she pursues a new life and a new relationship.

Two people must take the time to work through all dynamics of their relationship. Taking the time to know each other, taking the time to make decisions about moving in together — these are essentials when two people plan to spend a life together. Many of life's events and emotions require time to be understood and to be incorporated into the fabric of daily living.

This discussion of the grieving process has been done from the perspective of only one person; often, both parties in a new relationship will be suffering from the process at the same time, as they break emotionally from their former lovers or spouses. The matter is complicated even further because both are probably not at the same stage in the process nor do both necessarily possess the same ability to deal with it effectively.

If all of these factors are at work in a relationship, then a high degree of honesty and trust is required for success in working through these substantial barriers to closeness.

The rewards of "sticking to it" are many. It is often easier to quit than to continue. Continuance means struggle, patience, and often pain; but it also results in trust, intimacy, maturity, wisdom, understanding, and deep levels of personal, emotional, and spiritual growth. The result can be a covenant between two individuals that endures for a lifetime. Forever *is* a possibility. The old romantic goals are achievable — but not necessarily through the old romantic myths. Two people can have whatever they want if they identify the need, commit themselves to resolving problems rather than quitting, and pursue their goal together.

Separate But Equal

"Falling in love" ultimately means a lasting relationship between two people. The accent is on the "two." There exists a lot of common language in our myth of relationships which suggests that two people become, in fact, one person. Rather than a statement about the bonding process, or the consequences of a mutual covenant, what is often meant by this phrase is that one person becomes absorbed into the identity of the other.

Women perhaps best understand this problem, as they have for generations been subjugated socially to the will and identity of their husbands. Unfortunately, gay men and women have often fallen into this trap of tradition as well. More often than I care to remember, I have heard one person say, "She is mine" or "He is mine." A healthy covenant relationship does not involve rights of possession.

Time and again, one person may dominate a relationship so much that the other person loses a sense of dignity, self-worth and even identity. The spouse becomes merely an appendage or a shadow of the other. How often have you heard, or maybe even said yourself, "This is my other half" or "This is my better half," as if implying that one is not a whole person without the other?

Surely, we affirm that the one partner adds a dynamic and a dimension to the other which neither wishes to relinquish. Surely, the complementary giving and receiving does bring out the best in each other. Nevertheless, a healthy relationship is composed of two individuals who remain autonomous — independent and complete without the other. This allows for such a rich blending of talent and difference that the resulting couple becomes even more dynamic.

The "two become one" only in commitment and covenant, not in personality. "This is my spouse" means only covenant — not possession. All of this requires a maturity and a movement toward freedom and liberation which is the essential ingredient in any relationship. Being liberated to love is the goal of our striving.

The phrase "separate but equal" points to independent, yet mutually shared, decisions regarding household chores, living arrangements, financial management, sexual expression, religion and spirituality, social commitments, and a host of other facets of life.

Choosing to spend time apart may be as important as choosing to spend time together. What do you do when one person wants to go to a social function and the other does not? Can you compromise? Can one stay at home or go elsewhere without being "guilt-tripped" by the other? How often do we say, "If you love me, you'll go with me" or "Everybody expects you to go with me"?

How often do we expect our spouse to fulfill the expectations of our co-workers as to their role? The "corporate wife" syndrome affects many couples, making the spouse merely an attachment for fulfilling social expectation or requirements for promotion and advancement.

It becomes even more complex for gay and lesbian couples to live in this tension and try to fulfill the expectation of others. Often, we try to accommodate until the cost of accommodation begins to destroy our relationship and the identity of both partners. The attempt to merge one life into the expectations of another is difficult enough without the complications caused by the expectations of the boss, friends, family, the church, and others.

Often, then, both identities get lost in the accommodation effort. If this persists over time without being questioned, two people can drift slowly apart without even realizing what happened or how.

The goal of a relationship is the healthy union of two separate persons, and the joining together of gifts, talents, skills, histories, life perspectives, religious traditions, value systems, and personality. This can be done with joy and excitement in ways that can preserve and protect the uniqueness of each person. The desired result is a couple who collectively express a model of unity, mutuality, friendship, trust, and individuality which enriches the lives of friends and family.

This is the goal of every union. It does not matter if the couple is traditionally heterosexual or gay or lesbian; the only difference is that gay people have more barriers than our friends in the non-gay world. But, if approached positively, this factor can actually build strength in our relationships.

The achievement of equality and the maintenance of a relationship that involves dignity, self-worth, value, and self-esteem for one another depends on the development of relationship skills that can enable two persons to discover, cement and unite in a relationship with the possibility of creating a long-term successful lifetime union.

If we have any hope of increasing the longevity of gay relationships, we must develop these relationship skills.

4

Relationship skills

Starting from Scratch

The prerequisite skills necessary for good, clean and honest communication are gravely absent from American culture. As children we were not taught to express our feelings or to state our desires openly. The rules of our culture had much more to do with what we couldn't say than what we could. Not only were we discouraged from open expressions of ourselves, some areas of communication were, and are, actually taboo.

I grew up in an environment in which sex was simply not discussed. It was as though it did not exist. References to sex were always muted. This is common and, although the unspoken barrier is breaking down in places and among some groups of enlightened people, we still find that the subject is not frequently a topic of accepted discussion.

46

Attempts to express honest feeling, to vent fear, anger and gut-level emotions, were, and still are, met with negative and disapproving responses. Getting angry was not considered appropriate and was even devalued morally, being labeled as "un-Christian." "Daddy's little boy doesn't cry" has haunted many a male for whom the venting of emotion gave rise to serious questioning of his masculinity. Conversely, a young woman was not to desire or to enjoy the rough-and-tumble freedom of her brother lest her femininity be challenged.

In the proscriptive society in which we were raised, we were encouraged to develop rugged individualism. Becoming self-reliant and self-sufficient, the self-made man (note that women were not driven to be self-made) was the coveted American dream. As much as I appreciate the cultural values of independence, this perpetual goal only hurts a person's ability to relate socially. Our energy was channeled into hiding our feelings and toward an attitude of "I can do it alone."

This is admittedly a simple overview, but it carries much truth. The American male is bred to be rugged, self-reliant, and a near-automaton while the female is bred to be dependent upon the male. This is no foundation for developing relationship skills.

Let me define the term "relationship skills" as I use it here. These are the skills required for two or more persons to effectively communicate their feelings, ideas, desires, needs, fears, and other emotions in a context that is mutually supportive and free of judgment. A relationship built around such skills will enhance the self-esteem of each person in it.

If this is the desired goal, then it is clear that the American socialization process is in direct conflict with the goal. Men and women in our society are just not well equipped to relate at the level I am suggesting. We are starting from scratch as we discuss relationship skills and try to incorporate them into our lives. From what we have learned of successful relationships, it seems that we have had to jettison previously held values and behavior to start and maintain those relationships effectively.

If it is difficult for heterosexual men and women to build successful relationships, how much more challenging it is for gay men and women to build a relationship when we consider that the social model we grew up with was designed to make a "happy" heterosexual marriage. If the system does not work well for our friends in the non-gay community, it is indeed bankrupt for us.

What we often see in gay relationships can be simplified as follows: for the gay woman, having been raised to expect to find her identity in a husband (perhaps even being prepared to submerge that identity in that of her mate), she suddenly discovers that as a single woman or as part of a lesbian couple, she must exercise the aggressive, self-reliant attributes she was not supposed to learn. Role conflicts often develop or, worse, are avoided or denied as the lesbian mates both attempt to fit into a dominant/passive heterosexual model. This occurs time again without either woman realizing what is happening or that this self-constricting model does not work for their non-gay friends either.

Conversely, two men raised to be strong, aggressive, and self-reliant discover great conflicts as they merge their lives in a gay relationship. It is the collision of two worlds evolved from the premise that they are not supposed to unite. The ego crash is often gigantic. Again, what happens too often is that one party adopts the submissive role and tries to copy the heterosexual American model.

I am not saying that a person growing up in America cannot learn these skills. It can be done, as those who have successfully escaped the trap have taught us. Nonetheless, far too many gay people are allowing themselves to be limited by the models of others.

We must be willing to move beyond the bias and limitations of our cultural heritage in order to develop relationships. This is essential whether we are building a bonded, coupled union or a nation. We must start anew with confidence and hope — not with bitterness and rebellion.

Compromise

The growth, health and longevity of a relationship requires that we each be willing to reconsider our positions, move out of our accustomed ways of doing things, and become open to another's viewpoint, another's behavior, even another's way of living. Being locked into sex roles articulated by our culture prohibits that movement toward one another. Coming together creates a new entity in which the couple begins to put together its own symbols of life and its meaning. The relationship becomes a new entity — a third party in effect. There is "you," and there is "me"; and then there is "us." "The two of us" is something more — a power and a new dynamic is created when the "two of us" come together.

Compromise is giving up a portion of one "way" or opinion to allow the inclusion of another. A major barrier to compromise is simply that of poor communication. Both parties in a relationship must learn to listen or to hear one another if compromises are to occur. Here is an illustration from my own experience. It is a two-part game that enables the players to gain basic knowledge of each other. This is how Alan and I played it.

In the first section, I asked Alan to describe his family's habits and customs around eating dinner. They always, with rare exceptions, ate at home. Alan's mother cooked and all meals were normally eaten at her table. Going out to dinner was both rare and considered economically extravagant. Then follows my response: my family ate out very often, especially on Sunday. It was normal to ask "where shall we eat" along with "what shall we eat." I never thought a thing about it. Conclusion: playing the first part of this game uncovered a basic lifestyle difference between us and explained why Alan got upset by my perennial question "where shall we eat?" To him, it was not a reasonable question since the assumed answer was: "at home, of course." Knowing this fundamental difference between us revealed much about why dinner out often became uncomfortable and the basis for argument. Neither of us understood the family value system beneath our divergent feelings on this simple subject. The result of the game was a lessening of tension around something so basic as mealtime, a new appreciation of the other's traditions and, consequently, more meals at home for me and more meals out for Alan — together, of course! Compromise. We learned to talk out our deep internal feelings; the mystery about what was really going on between us dissipated.

Part two of the game involved our sharing of how our families spent their vacation time. Alan's family spent its vacations in the mountains camping out; mine was spent at the beach and *never* camping. It sounds classic, but true. From this I learned that I was putting a very negative value on the camping-out tradition and therefore putting down Alan and his family. We still don't camp and perhaps never will, but I no longer see it in such a negative light. The attitude of "I will never do such a thing," with all its implied arrogance, thus passes — allowing us to feel a greater mutual respect.

It is not possible, in my opinion, for two persons to live together for any length of time without having to give up some individual ways of doing things for the sake of the mutual agreement and the preservation of healthy communication. This may sound so basic as not to deserve mention, yet all too often I observe two people in conflict who refuse to consider the other's experiences. Communication is virtually shut down or perhaps it never really started. This is one of the points at which the temptation to quit is stronger than the challenge to stay. Often, gay men and women have spent many years learning to live alone and creating our own independent lifestyles; it is hard to change these behavior patterns. Merging two lives and two households creates a collision of two worlds. To survive, compromise is essential.

One key to compromise is to discover how you got your ideas about what you want; this brings up the unsettled issue of the "shopping list lover." Many of our ideas about living together are merely composites of other people's standards. One composite is influenced primarily by the behavior and standards of our parents and families. If both persons in a relationship are aware of this ever-present dynamic, they will be better able to perceive their differences and to acknowledge and address them. This process of recognizing differences is a critical component of compromise.

The result of compromise is, happily, drawing together. Drawing together in union leads to the next step of a growing relationship: contracts and agreements.

Contracts and Agreements

Terms like "contracts" and "agreements" sound like they belong to the world of business rather than being terms used to discuss a relationship with a spouse. But we need to view our personal relationships with the same seriousness we demand from business partners.

When we address the question of contracts and agreements, we get beyond this barrier. How can we expect a relationship to last, to be forever, unless we realize that longevity is a product of the time, energy, and commitment we invest in a relationship? Investment is a good choice of words, for it is exactly what we are doing — we are investing in each other's lives. As much care and thought should go into this investment as goes into any other.

In some form or another, couples consciously need to establish the agreements or contracts of their relationship. These are especially important for gay and lesbian couples. Since there is little social support for our relationships, a clear mutual understanding of expectaions is paramount.

Far too many people fall into the trap of making untrue assumptions ending in mutual hurt and disappointment. All of us make assumptions about ourselves and others; these need to be examined. This examination provides a good foundation for making agreements.

What are the agreements I am discussing here? Agreements are mutual. They require the consent of both parties in the relationship. They can be for any length of time. It is important to note that agreements may *need* to change with time and as circumstances of the relationship change. We have all noticed what happens to a plant when it is not repotted over a long period of time: it gets root-bound and literally stops growing. So, too, relationships are living organisms which need to grow.

An agreement does not need to be a written document, sealed, signed, and notarized — although it can be. One danger in committing your agreement to writing is that one of you may use it as the binding "law." The purpose of an agreement is to clarify the relationship and to give life to the couple, not to constrict, bind or entrap. Agreements represent the achievement of clear and honest communication. Honesty is necessary in any agreement; without it even the law recognizes that there is no agreement at all.

Another important dimension is that it is okay for agreements to change. The process is the same; both parties mutually and honestly agree to simply change the rules. I like to use the term "contracting" for the process I describe. Contracting incorporates mutual pledges and commitments, the articulation of shared and divergent expectations, and honesty which seeks to find specifics and eliminate ambiguity.

Keeping in mind the pitfalls of legalism, it may be helpful to commit your contract to writing. It should not be too complex, but it needs to encompass all of the areas which may produce conflict within the relationship.

Contracts can be made about anything: from who cooks and shops, to who does the washing and ironing, to how money is managed. But the largest area of conflict requiring some agreement is sex. Any agreements in the tender area of sexuality must be based on an understanding of certain principles:

1. Each of us has standards or expectations about the role of sex in a relationship. These emanate from a number of external sources, most notably parents and religion.
2. Each of us has different sexual needs and desires.
3. No person will be able to fulfill our sexual needs all the time.
4. We will not be able to fulfill our partner's sexual needs all the time.
5. Being honest about our needs and fantasies is most important in order to reach agreement.

There is the issue of sex: is our relationship exclusive or not? Is it open or closed? This is a hot issue; it must be honestly addressed. My experience has been that a couple's first approach to the question is often to avoid it entirely by reaching for standard and traditional norms. What are these? Simply that a person must only have sex with their lover or spouse. This response must be broken down into its components: A. To whom does the tradition speak? B. What is the motive behind the choice? C. What is the definition of "open" in the term "open relationship"? Let's look at these questions in more detail.

To whom does the tradition speak? Our Western Judeo-Christian mores regarding marriage and sex have historically existed for three reasons: first, to govern the behavior of women rather than men (i.e., Biblical teaching about adultery defines the behavior of women alone); second, to control the family lineage, as it was deemed important to know who was whose father; and third, to reinforce and give religious sanction to the needs of growing economic and industrial states.

Most of us were therefore raised with the ethical perspective that sex is only for heterosexually married persons. To this has been added the further dimension of procreation. These considerations do not take into account gay and lesbian relationships.

What is the motive behind the choice of open versus closed relationships? Given this Judeo-Christian heritage, we often feel a compulsion to be exclusive in a relationship because it is "right," "expected," "Christian" or the like. This is a very sensitive point. To choose an exclusive, closed relationship is possible and valid if both parties honestly want to make that choice. It is perfectly acceptable, even in the lesbian and gay world, to elect a monogamous relationship and it is a healthy, responsible choice — but only if it is the clear and unequivocal selection of both participants in the relationship.

My experience has been that most couples make the choice not freely but out of obligation, guilt and fear. They feel obligated to choose it since it is universally sanctioned. They feel guilt about many unresolved and uncommunicated issues regarding their own sexuality and, hence, cover their guilt with a legalistic choice. And couples make this choice out of fear that they may otherwise lose their partner if they entertain or suggest any other option. The fear motive is a major factor in this issue and raises the question,

"What is an open relationship?"

First, it is important to understand the term "open" relationship is a highly subjective one: everyone means something slightly different by it. I have never met anyone who had a self-professed open relationship in which there were no limitations — no agreements as to the terms of the openness which would be assumed or which permitted a sexual liaison anywhere, anytime. The couples I have known and worked with professionally have had a variety of rules about the expectations of one another sexually and all have had restrictions.

This is the most volatile area of agreements; it requires a great deal of honesty to address the subject with your partner. What happens when you say, "I think I want to go to bed with another?" Is this a major crisis or can you both face the honest feelings?

Honesty requires trust. Facing these honest exchanges with one another is a test of the strength of love and trust as well as an opportunity to enhance and deepen the love relationship. To honestly confront this issue does not necessarily result in "outside" sexual experiences. Many times the mere freedom and love which allows the honest expression of the feelings are enough to fulfill a person's need. People who have complete freedom of choice often do not exercise that license.

Over the years in working with couples, I have been repeatedly asked to pronounce that they should have a closed relationship — as though it were an infallible principle. My response can only be that what matters is not being "open" or "closed" to outside sexual experiences; what matters is that two people reach an honest and trusting agreement about what they want and expect from each other and that they live by that agreement. Honesty and faithfulness to the agreement are the critical components. The word "faithfulness" has been used traditionally to mean sexual exclusivity. This is not my meaning here. Faithfulness is to be honest and to keep (i.e., be faithful to) the mutual agreement no matter the content of the agreement.

A part of the myth about our community is that the issue of open relationship affects only men, that women do not have open relationships. While it is probably true that women in America are socialized to be sexually exclusive with one man and that lesbians have often adopted the same standard for their relationships, my experience has also shown that more and more women are having successful open relationships and engaging in frequent sexual encounters with a kind of intensity often attributed only to men.

The deeper question regarding sexuality is this: why do we seek to define the entire relationship by what happens sexually? We have historically defined marriage and fidelity around sexuality. I believe that we do this out of a desire to control and channel sexual expression. Why do we want to control it?

The answer is that many people are afraid of sexuality. We have never adequately positioned sex in our society. It plays an inordinate role, dominating our lifestyle. We fear sex because of this relationship with power. Every sexual encounter incorporates a mutual exchange of power in an erotic context. Power is an appropriate term here because it both touches the reality of experience of sex and leads us toward a deeper experience of intimacy and, ultimately, a new confrontation with our inherent spirituality.

Sexuality is a powerful and volatile energy within each of us. Its very power has caused us to seek its control. We have placed moral and religious sanctions around our sexuality like walls, to insure that our sexual energies not be unleashed. We have used a multitude of psychological devices to proscribe and diagnose sexual behavior. Such forces were, for years, the basis for the diagnosis of homosexuality as a disorder.

I believe that this massive social effort to structure sexual expression stems from a fear of sex itself. Thus, fear arises from an encounter with the power and energy of sexual expression. At the core of our being lies a sexual energy which, when tapped, leads us into levels of spiritual awareness not generally acknowledged in our culture. We will explore this phenomenon when we discuss sexuality and spirituality in a gay relationship.

Looking back over the whole issue of developing relationship skills, we encounter several factors which together contribute to building an effective relationship. Let us once more look at these factors.

Ties That Bind

There is an old Christian hymn called "Blessed Be the Tie That Binds." The ties that bind are the often neglected instruments of compromise, contracting, and the forming of agreements. Our culture has not equipped us with the tools necessary to create these instruments, even though they are the substance of success as we build our relationships.

The development of these skills should be a primary goal of all couples. I believe gay and lesbian couples especially need them because of the negative social forces working against our relationships. Two persons engaged in pursuit of a relationship should begin by seriously looking at their individual expectations (shopping lists), should pursue a course of counseling with a qualified counselor, and should commit themselves to taking the time to learn about one another.

Over the past several years I have developed a process for discerning the ties that bind. This process has produced both clarity and strength in the building stages of a new relationship; it involves a group workshop session with as many as a dozen couples. Here, we begin the process of asking honest questions about our relationships. If we have a dozen couples, we have at least twenty-four separate histories with distinct ideas about what it means to be in a relationship. The goal is not to mold the participants into one view but to acknowledge that the diversity is there.

The workshop experience is followed by at least three separate counseling sessions between an individual couple and the counselor. These sessions focus upon: (1) family relationships; (2) coming out; (3) personal histories; (4) conflict resolution; (5) financial management; (6) cohabitation; (7) sexual contracts; and any other factors that may arise during our discussions. The sessions are spaced at least two weeks apart; the spacing is most important and highlights again the value of taking time for this process.

Consider this image of the process: counseling is like plowing a field. All soil contains a multitude of creatures, seeds, spores, and hidden life forms which have been buried and packed down by time and pressure. To plow the soil is to loosen it, to aerate it, to allow moisture to penetrate it. This process starts things growing. Time is required to allow the buried seeds and spores to sprout. When they have sprouted, one is amazed at the mixture of flowers and weeds.

So too, a counseling session can disturb long-buried pieces of one's life. The time between sessions is a sprouting time in which these seeds from the past become visible and identified; they are thus available for cultivation or extermination.

Often a couple will return to me after a counseling session to recount a major argument which occurred some time after the previous session. The discussions had apparently disgorged some previously hidden or unacknowledged bit of energy, the discovery of which disrupted their daily patterns. A common response is to seek to avoid this process, to attempt to live together in union without ever returning to the past pains or to the buried memories. But life itself, with all its stresses, acts as a plow; it will ultimately invade and uncover all the buried debris of the past. Should not a couple proceed with a careful and loving guided approach to this excavation rather than subject their lives to the unpredictable invading forces of life?

The differences between the two approaches is the difference between an intentional, defined, methodical approach and the undisciplined, destructive assault of life forces. The primary problem with the passive approach of allowing life just to happen is twofold: first, it puts the individual and the couple in a passive posture and at the mercy of life forces rather than in control; second, it tends to confuse real issues such that our ability to distinguish one issue from another is severely impaired. Further, careful, mutual consideration of a troubling issue in a deliberate and loving way tends to eliminate the possibility that a later involuntary encounter with the problem will drive the couple to flee from it — and, hence, the relationship — since to flee may seem more appealing than working it out.

I do not believe that any relationship should be exempt from counseling forever. At one time or another, counseling will enhance the quality of life. Consider this medical analogy:

Modern radiotherapy (radiation) treatment is able to pinpoint and control the deposit of radioactive energy in a tissue in such a way that almost all of the desired energy is placed in the malignant tissue while leaving adjacent tissue untouched. This control achieved by modern technology replaces much earlier techniques which literally blasted a gross area of the body with a dose of radiation.

In a like manner, counseling is a form of therapy that seeks to pinpoint the issue or issues that threaten the well-being of an individual or a relationship. Therapy offers a defined approach as contrasted with the "blast" effect of the life process we all share. The blast effect of life will still happen and nothing we can do will eliminate that; however, counseling can control the energy of the blast. Like modern radiotherapy, energy is placed at the point of the problem rather than scattered indiscriminately throughout the life system.

The key to a successful relationship is not a mystery. We do not need to be at the mercy of life's vagaries; we can activate the relationship skills within us to avoid the disastrous effect of an undirected life course. We can learn to employ these tools to cultivate our individual and shared gifts.

We do not live at the whim of some serendipitous Cupid who slings arrows randomly. We can learn to develop relationship skills so that our lives will be clear signs of success to encourage others, to symbolize hope and to attain levels of mental, physical and emotional health previously thought to be outside of the capability of gay men and lesbians.

5

True stories
from gay relationships

At this point, it may be useful to look at real-life relationships to illustrate these points and to underscore the need for appropriate ways to affirm, celebrate and symbolize with integrity our gay relationships.

"Shot Gun" Holy Union

This incident is reminiscent of that related earlier of the young man in Dallas, Texas, who called Rev. Eastman expressing his state of being "in love" with his new acquaintance of but a few days. My phone rang late one night. A young man urgently wanted to discuss how soon he and his lover could "get married." The conversation was interspersed with whispers from the background, and occasional laughter and giggles from another invading the speaker's comments. I was convinced that these two men were in bed, having interrupted their ardent lovemaking long enough to call a preacher.

Normally, this situation would have angered me, especially in view of the post-midnight hour; but on this occasion I decided merely to join in their game. I began asking the caller questions. How long have you been together? "Since New Year's Eve," was the reply. It was now January 2. I followed with a series of further questions about knowing one another, jobs, family, where they would live, work, etc. The caller began to change his tone from the calm, amorous tone to a more serious questioning. A tinge of doubt began to creep into his responses. He began to tell his partner, "Stop, I am talking with the preacher." The conversation ended with his thanking me for pointing out a few questions which needed answering and his telling his friend to get dressed. After I hung up the phone, I could not contain my laughter since I could then fully imagine what was going on as these two began to ask serious questions about their non-existent future plans.

I have never been able to understand the urgent need for a Holy Union.

Another call came from a woman who insisted that she and her lover be "married" by Saturday since her lover was going away for three years on a remote tour of duty in the service. My response to her, which seriously questioned the need for a covenant between two people who had never lived together and who would not see one another for three years, fell on unresponsive ears. My personal concern after this brief conversation was that the caller wanted some form of "insurance policy" that would literally guarantee her lover's return to her, and that would forbid her lover to engage in sex with another woman while away for three years.

Blood Tests?

A couple called me to ask about a Holy Union. One of their first questions was a request to direct them to the proper authorities for a marriage license, followed by a query as to whether blood tests were required. Blood tests required by any jurisdiction as part of an application for a marriage license are only relevant to heterosexual couples and relate to their procreative intent. That a gay couple should ask this question as well as inquire about the necessity of a marriage license only emphasizes the extent to which we have adopted wholesale the structures and symbols inappropriate to our experience. The impulse to mimic heterosexual customs and norms carries with it a denial of one's selfhood, unique reality, and liberty.

I was completely taken aback and disturbed by these questions. My disturbance at the way gay and lesbian couples view themselves provided much of the impetus for this book.

Make Believe

In the early 1970s, I observed many occasions in which lesbian and gay couples participated in Holy Unions which looked for all the world like traditional heterosexual marriages. The painstaking measures adopted by these couples even included such extremes as one of the (male) partners wearing a long white wedding gown and the other a tuxedo. These extravaganzas were attended by bridesmaids, flower girls, ring-bearers and the throwing of rice. It made no difference whether the couple was two men or two women; the outward symbols would be the same.

I am always amazed at our inability to question these symbols. For example, the tradition of throwing rice originated as a fertility rite to express the hope that the couple would bear many children. This is, of course, grossly out of place in a gay union. The fact that gay couples may adopt children or make other arrangements for raising children in the relationship is unrelated to the cultural act of rice-throwing. There are certainly other symbols we can create to embody our relationships and their expression of family.

To choose every traditional symbol is to deny or diminish our own creativity and ability to symbolize our history in ways that communicate the reality of our relationships. The task before us is to identify those symbols that are embedded in traditional rites which *do* embody a universal reality of relationship and to liberate these symbols from their cultural content and employ them in new ways. Such an endeavor can produce both beauty and power in the celebration of our unions.

My Husband, My Wife?

Following this same pattern of conformity with society's images of the marriage, I have had more than a handful of couples strive to identify one partner as the "husband" and the other as the "wife." This trend appeared initially to be merely a slang expression among gay couples; however, when challenged, a couple is often adamant that one is the husband and the other the wife. They are unwilling to entertain any other symbolic identification and seem locked into a pattern of total conformity.

The most extreme example I have witnessed of this phenomenon was that of two women who insisted that they occupied the respective positions of husband and wife and who lived in a predominantly heterosexual social structure and disconnected from the gay community, even to the point of the "husband" maintaining a fully male identity (in name and in all other outward ways). Neither was transsexual. Rather, this seemed to be an intensely felt role adoption which maintained for them the pretense — through a denial of their homosexuality — of conventionality.

The transformation of gay and lesbian behavior in the late 1970s indicates a breaking away from social conformity in the symbolization of our relationships. Chapter Seven sets forth a contemporary format for the symbolization, affirmation and celebration of our relationships which integrates both our sexuality and our spirituality. This integration is the essential task if we are to achieve wholeness in our relationships.

"I Shot Her!"

One issue addressed in the process of relationship counseling is the way two people resolve conflict. A colleague of mine shared with me the story of one of his counseling assignments. He had asked a couple individually about their former relationships and how they were resolved. The response of one partner to the question, "How did you resolve the conflict you have been speaking about with your former lover?" was "I took a gun and shot her."

While I am unsure of the kind of response I could make to this shocking statement, I am confident that, when feelings are submerged, they eventually erupt in violent and unproductive ways. I am also convinced that relationship skills can go a long way to eliminate destructive eruptions of emotions. Anger can be a constructive and useful emotion when focused and used to articulate honest feeling. When turned inward or avoided, it can result in the violent end that befell the ill-fated former lover above.

Years in the Making

A more positive story of relationships is offered in the experience of two women who had been together for several years and came to me for counseling. Over a period of three or more years, we attempted to move toward the celebration of their union. At every meeting, there seemed to arise an issue upon which neither could reach agreement. It was both a serious and humorous experience as they would each time abruptly leave my office with the consensus that "We had better go home and talk this out." The issues to be resolved varied from the completion of a legal divorce for one of the women to the guest list at the Holy Union. As frustrating as the experience may have been for the participants (and for me, as I witnessed the almost eternal approach and slow resolution of every conceivable issue), it is testimony to their patience, devotion, perseverance, and growth that, one by one, each issue was faced and resolved.

The celebration of their Holy Union was a joy for them, and even more so, for their friends who had witnessed their struggles. There was truly a sense of victory and achievement as their lives and relationship embodied hope for their friends.

Holiday Cycles

Over many years of observing relationships in our community, I have discovered some notable and predictable cycles. Unfailingly at Christmastime, just prior to Valentine's Day, and in the perennial wedding month of June, couples will call me asking for a Holy Union. There is, of course, nothing wrong with scheduling the celebration of a union during these times and it is part of our socialization process to want to join our historical family and cultural celebrations with the celebration of our relationships. It is important, however, to be aware of the cycles and the dynamics that influence our decisions in this respect.

Often, couples choose to celebrate their union at times which coincide with family tradition, old anniversaries and previous relationship cycles. However, the cycles should be recognized so that we can better cope with the possibility that we will not "get our way." Because of the cycle effect, we can expect several couples to ask for celebrations at the same time, and at least some of the petitioners will be disappointed in the choice of available dates. The result is but another opportunity to look at one's motivations and at the need to take time to arrive at a final decision. The best advice for a couple in the early stages of their relationship is to "go slowly" and take things one day at a time. It is not uncommon for a couple to begin talking about a Holy Union after only a few weeks of dating. This sense of urgency is destructive to the health of a relationship. It often emerges at holidays and anniversaries as people try to recapture the past and tie it to the present as a way of finding continuity and affirmation. The deeper motivating factors here are insecurity and fear of loss. These factors must be addressed in order to maintain perspective.

Let's Do It Alone

Increasingly, couples are approaching me for a celebration of their relationship involving just the two of them alone. The couple may be new to an area and have few or no intimate friends with whom they would want to share the special moment of a Holy Union. It is difficult to discover the motivation here or to decide whether this is wise.

The key is to assure that the couple is not merely avoiding the need for community and social support. A relationship cannot be lived in a vacuum, however closeted the participants may be. The relationship affects and is affected by family and friends; it is imperative to explore the role of family and friends in the celebration itself.

Too many times, I have seen a couple withdraw from the world and seek to relate only to one another as though they alone were enough for one another and needed no one else. This works for only a short period and usually ends in major conflict as the partners discover they need support and nurture. Frequently, the discovery comes after anger, pain and resentment have built up. If our lives are lived in community, then it is crucial that the celebration of our unions be shared in community; such celebrations, after all, are a focal point of the interpretation of the meaning of our lives. Such an event cannot be solitary.

Three's a Crowd

It is true that couples occasionally share sexual experiences with a third person, or even with several others. Couples also have close intimate relationships with others. These may involve love, sex, and significant bonding, but they are not often long-term relationships.

I have known people who have formed three-party bonding. My experience indicates that this is not in the long term a "successful configuration." The coupling need in humans is extremely strong and results in both primary and secondary relationships. A three-person relationship will almost inevitably result in two people forming a primary relationship and the other being a secondary. I will admit that this is merely my personal bias; it is, however, formed by both experience and knowledge of the dynamics of pair bonding. The commitment, energy and time needed to create a long-term, healthy pair-bonding is enormous. I cannot see such energy being equally focused in three directions.

In my experience, the motivation behind three-party bonding is often to avoid the deep commitment levels called for in pair bonding. Another result of three-party bonding is a confusion of symbols being presented to family, friends and community. This resulting ambiguity can tend to isolate the triad and hinder individual growth. For triads that seek to work in community leadership capacities, the triad itself becomes a major barrier to effectiveness. A case in point is one in which a clergyperson serving gay men and lesbians was being considered for a position as pastor of a congregation. The process of consideration was terminated by the congregation when they were confronted with the potential pastor's three-way relationship. The lifestyle issue became paramount, eclipsing substantive issues of the person's qualifications for leadership. Perhaps this would not have represented a good match of pastor and congregation in any event; the fact remains that we cannot dismiss the impact of the apparently all-important lifestyle issue.

I am not advocating that we make choices based upon what the community can or will accept; if that were the case, the entire thesis of this book would be jeopardized. But we cannot be naïve about the effects of our choices. In the case of three-party bonding, the effects often undermine one's ability to provide community leadership. This reality is just another of the many stresses placed upon the triad in addition to the complicated and difficult dynamics of the relationship itself.

All of these circumstances and real-life situations show the varied dynamics of our bonding and the need for a serious, hopeful and aggressive approach to our relationships. Even the absurd realities which seem far outside our own experience can cause us to look more seriously at our own motivations in forming relationships.

In the end, let us look at the interpretation of these situations. Let us address the act of celebration of gay and lesbian pair bonding. What is the role of sexuality? What does a Holy Union and a Rite of Blessing look like? What does it mean to "bless a relationship"? How might the blessing change or alter the relationship?

These are social, cultural, spiritual and theological issues that face our community. Our task is to create structures and symbols that will express our unions in such a way as to resolve the present social/theological conflict that inhibits the growth and self-esteem of gay and lesbian couples. We must assault this conflict with an emerging ethic that answers not just society's questions but our own as well. In so doing, we can restore wholeness to gay people and redeem our histories from social insignificance. So great a challenge demands the full use of our vast spiritual and personal gifts. Without our fundamental positive energy, self-image, self-love, and genuine power, such an agenda would not be achievable. These resources are ours to claim.

With this affirmation, let us look at the symbolization and celebration of our unions.

6

Holy Unions
and Rites of Blessing

The Essential Task: Gay Spirituality

Many readers may consider themselves to be basically non-religious. Nonetheless, we need to explore the central images our culture uses to interpret relationships. None of us can escape the Judeo-Christian symbols that pervade our social structures and influence our moral beliefs. There are spiritual and theological components of our task of affirmation; to explore those we at least need to understand the context out of which our inherited symbols have emerged.

Let's begin with an important generalization: *Our culture has gone to great lengths to separate sexuality and spirituality.* We do not think of spirituality ever expressing sexuality; we may, in fact, use spirituality to control sexual energy. Our culture is obsessed with sexual imagery; it employs that imagery even in the marketplace, while at the same time reinforcing many taboos regarding sexual expression.

This sexual-spiritual split affects us all. Gay men and lesbians in particular are keenly aware of this split and probably have a tendency to accept it without question. Non-gay people tend to believe that traditional marriage is the point of union between spirituality and sexuality. While this certainly is true for some, the vast majority of our population uses marriage as the controlling force to bind sexuality. We note the lack of sexual imagery in most Western religious rites; sexual images appear only after they have been spiritualized and never include genital reference. This results from a negative cultural attitude about the body and its sexual organs.

I grew up in an environment that placed inordinate energy into the denial of sexuality. I never heard it discussed except in whispered tones and disguised language away from the ears of the children. I never saw a naked human body other than my own until I was in my late teens.

The message that sex is bad or dirty is communicated to us through vehicles like these. At the core of this communication network is a set of religious symbols that add a negative value judgment to the topic of sexuality.

I vividly recall a roommate of mine in college. During summer school, on one very hot August night, he put on a pair of long-sleeved flannel pajamas before going to bed. It was not his custom to do so; but he was getting married in two months and he mentioned that he needed to learn to wear pajamas. I was so shocked at the implications of this statement that I couldn't even muster an answer.

My roommate was saying that it was improper for a man to allow his wife to see him naked. He clearly believed that sex was a necessary evil which should not be enjoyed or discussed openly. This incident underscores in my mind the profound need for us to overcome the sexual-spiritual split in order to establish healthy attitudes with regard to our bodies, genital organs, and sexuality.

It is surprising that the central image and event of Christian religion is stated in terms like "And the Word became flesh, full of grace and truth." (John 1:14, RSV). It certainly appears to me that the Christian church has not yet fully understood the radical meaning of these words. This Biblical proclamation reminds us that the "Word" — i.e., God, spiritual reality — has been immersed in human flesh. The verse further proclaims that the flesh embodied truth. If truth is part of our spiritual development, we must know the truth of the flesh in union with spirit.

Another Biblical text, from the Old Testament, reads: "It shall come to pass afterward that I will pour out my spirit on all flesh." (Joel 2:28, RSV). This often-quoted phrase must be explored. It does not say that God will pour out God's spirit on *some* flesh, or on *male* flesh, or that the spirit will stop at the neck or at the waist. No, it incorporates *all* human flesh.

Study of Biblical scripture reveals an abundance of sexual imagery which has been culturally screened or spiritualized to separate it from physical reality. What would be the reaction of people if, on a given Sabbath, their priest, rabbi, or minister told them that God's spirit dwells in their genitals and that their sexual exchange could be holy and a sacred experience? Only by imagining such an example is it possible to properly perceive how separated we have become from our sexual selves. True, most people would be appalled at such comments from their spiritual leader; but for the gay community this sexual-spiritual split has prevented us from becoming part of any organized spiritual community and indeed from being able to claim our own spirituality.

What is happening in America today is this: There is a new message going forth out of the old set of symbols. This message offers spiritual values to gay people. Everywhere, an energy is arising from gay spirituality; every major religious denomination has gay caucuses within it. This phenomenon was precipitated by the emergence and rapid growth of the Metropolitan Community Churches. Since 1968, this ministry to gay Christians has spread worldwide, radically challenging the Western concept of spirituality and sexuality.

The essential task of Western religion is to unite spirituality with sexuality; this should be on the agenda for all churches in the 1980s and 1990s. This task represents the teaching that sexuality is an honored gift from God. For centuries, gay people have been excluded and even thrown out of our churches and synagogues on the grounds that our sexual orientation is incompatible with religion. The irony of this new age of union between sexuality and spirituality is that the very reason for excluding homosexuals has been the vehicle for our return to faith. It is precisely our seeking to fulfill our lives and to understand our sexual identity that has brought many of us from the brink of being "unchurched" back to a discovery of our place in the Family of God. Our sexuality — the stumbling block for many churches — has become the occasion of our encounter with God's acceptance.

Lesbians and gay men now have a prophetic function to fulfill in the Judeo-Christian Western religious system. We are the point at which the union of sexuality and spirituality occurs. Consistent with the revelation that God always chooses a rejected people through whom to act, gay people are revealing the re-union of sexuality and spirituality. As we express our faith and relationship to our God, we are fulfilling revelation. Our very presence is a judgment upon the church as we visibly and physically embody the rejection of hundreds of thousands, even millions, of God's children. We are also grace as well as judgment as we embody the message of God's love and acceptance for all who are yet afraid — who hide within their fears.

It is not necessary at this point to address all the issues of Biblical interpretation that are frequently raised on this subject; it is not the purpose of this book to debate the Bible and its position on homosexuality. Such questions are adequately addressed from nearly every religious persuasion in dozens of books. We can, nonetheless, proclaim the good news that the

Scriptures, when studied carefully and with scholarship, offer no condemnation of homosexuality as we know it today. In fact, there is no discussions of sexual orientation within the Scripture; there are only accounts of abusive and idolatrous sexual practices, which are justifiably condemned.

Gay men and women of faith embody hope for all people, as we represent the union of sexuality and spirituality. As time goes by, leaders of established religious denominaions will have to reach out to the gay people they have excluded and seek our expertise in teaching their congregations to resolve fears and doubts over sexuality. As gay people, we are claiming our sexuality as a gift from God and using this "giftedness" to free our spirits. Again, the spiritual trust is this: that which was grounds for rejection (homosexuality) has become the occasion for acceptance.

The healing of the sexual-spiritual split is essential for all people if we seriously want to establish relationships, and most especially if we are to bless these relationships. The discovery of our spirituality in union with our sexuality has revealed to us that our relationships are no longer defined by sexual behavior but rather must be defined along lines of spiritual truth and deeper levels of intimacy. Far too many people, gay and non-gay alike, have become "stuck" at the level of genital sex. We must experience a sense of freedom regarding sex in order to move beyond our genital fixation. This, in turn, relates back to our lack of relationship skills, our problem of communication, and our lack of mutual honesty and trust.

Too often we use genital sex as a means to address or meet other needs. We ask a person to go home with us; we ask if they want to engage in a specific sexual activity, in order to meet deeper needs for intimacy and human touch. I recall a young man telling me that he would go home with people and have sex with them merely in order to be held, to be close to another, to avoid being alone for the night. These are inevitable human needs which often go unmet because we have not been taught relationship skills. What would happen if a person came up to you and said "Can I sleep with you tonight; I just want to be held" or "I don't want to be alone" or "I need intimacy"? Intimacy may include genital sex or it may not. We are so fixated on genital sex that we "require" an orgasm in order to feel fulfilled or completed. The often demeaned openness and freedom with which gay people engage in sexual activity may be the means for us to finally learn to go beyond orgasm to much deeper levels of intimacy. If orgasms and genital sexuality are available and frequent and stripped of their social, moral, and religious contaminants, then it may be easier for us to enjoy the varied levels of intimacy and the intensities of relationship which lie beyond the genital sexual experience.

I argue for openness and freedom only in the context of a responsible relationship that affirms the worth of each person. This context of openness requires special care if we are to avoid using one another both sexually and emotionally.

I am convinced that gay people have a major part

to play in achieving the essential task of healing our culture's attitudes toward sexuality. We are able to function in a prophetic role that shall enable us to understand the symbolization of our unions. To fully symbolize our unions (and create symbols for that purpose) requires that we confront sexual issues in order to freely express the dynamics of our relationships. Again, we must probe the religious symbols that rest near the heart of our value system.

Our task is not to destroy the Western Judeo-Christian value system but to redeem it, to free it from the social and cultural heritage that has stripped it of its power to embody life in its wholeness and, hence, life in its unity with God.

What Does It Mean To Bless A Relationship?
Blessing a relationship entails a resolution of the sexual-spiritual split, for every relationship is both a sexual and spiritual creature as well as a social and emotional one. To bless a relationship requires that no part of the relationship be omitted. If this is true — and I am certain that it is — then we face a serious religious crisis: we have, intentionally, omitted certain parts of the human relationship in our traditional rites of blessing. We have only included what society at the time deemed appropriate to bless. Much of life, much of our relationships, has been outside the circle of spiritual dominion. We have indeed *not* blessed more elements than we *have* blessed; we have judged much of life as separate from spirituality and we have worked hard at undoing the revelation that the Word

became flesh. We have therefore seriously damaged and dismantled the central doctrine of Christian faith: the incarnation. Now, let me be so bold as to say that gay and lesbian Christians are a major part of the restoration and the reformation of this damage. To understand this restoration, we must understand what it means to bless.

An image derived from an ancient story will speak to modern Jews and Christians and can become the vehicle for our reformation of relationships and the set of symbols which shall express those relationships. In the fourteenth chapter of the Book of Genesis, there is an account of a priest named Melchizedek, who is also a king. He in fact just appears and is called the King of Salem which means King of Peace. He thus has no recognized authority.

What happens in this story is quite amazing. Melchizedek meets Abraham. Abraham is the chief patriarch and the one whose life represents the life of all of God's people. When Melchizedek meets Abraham, who possesses much authority, Melchizedek blesses him and Abraham proceeds to give to Melchizedek a tenth of everything he has — he pays him a tithe. Here is a situation in which one who has no authority — the lesser of the two — presumes to bless him with greater authority and, even more incredibly, receives a gift from the greater. This transaction is the reverse of the usual Biblical protocol.

What happened? What was the blessing? The blessing was this: Melchizedek received Abraham, touched him, allowed him to come close and, in return, Abraham gave what he had. They received each other — that is, they acknowledged one another, symbolizing the mutual respect and authority by the exchange of the tithe. Melchizedek then gave Abraham the gift of bread and wine (note this foundation of the Christian sacrament of communion, the giving of bread and wine).

This account is further elaborated upon in Hebrews, Chapter Seven. Here, Jesus Christ is portrayed as a priest after the order of Melchizedek, which is a person without traditional authority to be a priest who instead exercises authority as direct from God. The exercise of this authority means to bless life by receiving life. This exchange is complete and inclusive of all life.

In the Western Catholic Church, the ordination of a priest has always included this reference to the priesthood of Melchizedek. In this grant of authority we find a previously unnoticed and essential ingredient for the liberties of all people. The only reference to the function of Melchizedek is to bless. Thus, the rite of blessing means to receive all life.

In 1969, I attended the musical play *Hair* in San Francisco. I was struck by an image on the cover of the Playbill which has remained with me since. It was the picture of a young androgynous person with arms spread wide in a dance form. To me, the picture communicated an embracing lifestyle, a posture ready to receive and accept life. It is this embracing and open lifestyle which enables blessing.

Now consider that the "normal" posture of people in our world is a defensive and protective one. We face life with our arms closed around us to protect us, to keep people away, and to hold on to our possessions. Here is the essential spiritual conflict: we are called to an embracing posture while the world advocates a defensive one. In the church, this defensive posture has produced the "defender of the faith" attitude and its consequent rejection of people, a refusal to embrace. This non-Biblical posture stands at the heart of the church's rejection of gay people, and this defensive posture further prevents the established religious orders from blessing gay relationships as well as the relationships of many other peoples. It is the inability to perceive this fundamental concept — that ministry must be given to all people of faith — that has caused the religious persecutions of our day. We must liberate the truth of this Biblical injunction from the perversion and non-practice of it by the historical church.

Our reformation, then, is found in the restoration of the Rite of Blessing — by taking on the authority given by *God*, rather than that credentialed through traditional modes.

Let us look at another passage from Hebrews: "For when there is a change in the priesthood, there is necessarily a change in the law as well." (Hebrews 7:12, RSV). I am advocating a change in the priesthood; the spiritual leaders of all religions must understand that the nature of their office is to bless. When this understanding has been reached, they will have won the freedom to receive and bless life, without the fear of reprisal from spiritual authorities, since the spiritual authority is that of Melchizedek who is without worldly authority. Scripture says that this is the nature of the authority of Christ as well. We therefore have a consistent and historical image of our mission to bless, a mission which has been universally misrepresented. Our reformation represents a return to this truth, an empowering of people, and a unique and specific witness that gay people are now at the vanguard of this revolution.

Rites of Blessing

Life lived to its fullest is a mutual give-and-take shared by all creatures. This reciprocity gives life, power, and unity and is itself a constant blessing. We are blessed and we bless as we receive the world around us. Hence, when we refuse to receive others — to acknowledge their life, worth, and essential human dignity — we withhold our blessing. A Rite of Blessing is a formal and intentional act of asking God to receive a person or a relationship. This act embodies and implies God's blessing as we are the agents of the blessing. It is we who receive — who act as priests and therefore use the authority given by God. In countless ways, our spiritual leaders have acted to bless relationships, things and events. It is time for them to bless gay relationships by receiving us into their fellowship. The symbol of this reception is simply a prayer acknowledging God's presence in, and embrace of, the relationship. This modest prayer need not be attended with many other customs.

Here, let us make a distinction between a Rite of Blessing and a Holy Union. The Rite of Blessing is the simple prayer which acknowledges the relationship and offers it to God as our Creator. The Holy Union is a contract or agreement, a covenant between two people reached after a significant period of life together.

It is appropriate to use the Rite of Blessing at various points in a couple's relationship: in the early beginning stages to symbolize its focus on spirituality; at the time of anniversaries to reinforce the growth achieved together in the pair-bonding process; and at other times that may benefit from focus upon essential relationship needs to affirm, celebrate and symbolize.

The Rite of Blessing is a useful tool that we, as gay men and women, can use to fill the void created when our religious institutions withhold rites of blessing and affirmation of our lifestyle.

The practice of this rite requires nothing more than the desire of two persons to acknowledge their spiritual bond, to recognize God's presence in their union and to symbolize the co-mingling of spirituality and sexuality. This rite is an underused act which can meet the needs of a relationship for affirmation prior to any contract agreement or covenant entered into in the form of a Holy Union.

Rites of Blessing are simple prayers which may be offered at any time and in any place; they need not require witnesses, vows, or an exchange of symbols. A Holy Union is much more complex.

Holy Union

A Holy Union contains within it the act and Rite of Blessing, yet it goes further by expressing a contract between two people. While a Rite of Blessing is a general act, the Rite of Holy Union is much more restricted. The intention of a Holy Union is to acknowledge the agreements of a couple who have explored their lives together, who have discussed and formulated a mutual covenant under which they seek to live. It is inadvisable for two people to seek a Holy Union without close examination and planning. This process is required *prior* to the union of two lives with the intention of maintaining this union throughout a lifetime. Every Holy Union carries with it the intention of pair bonding for life.

A Holy Union is a community event in which others significant to the couple share in the covenant ceremony. The symbol created by a Holy Union is one in which the community of faith (i.e., the church or synagogue) receives the witness of the couple's mutual agreement. The real blessing is their acknowledgment and reception of the couple as well as the couple's acknowledgment of the community. The two persons give themselves to their friends in what is a mutual blessing. At the core of this act is the simple prayer of blessing in which the agreement and transaction is offered to God. This somewhat simple symbolic act has been the center and source of great conflict within American religious communities.

In the early days of the Metropolitan Community

Churches, MCC congregations sought the use of other church facilities for worship and meetings. Often, other religious institutions and other American Christian denominations would offer MCC space to worship. This symbol of acceptance (Blessing) often included the restriction that Holy Unions could not be performed. Here, again, is evidence of the historic conflict between spirituality and sexuality. To perform a Holy Union implied that God would accept and bless such a union; this implication was not one the established churches wanted any part of. They were busy perpetuating the sexual-spiritual split and were not prepared to enter into dialogue over the issue of Holy Unions.

Here is the point at which gay men and lesbians are acting out their prophetic role in the church. Our Rites of Holy Union assault the church at the point of its own internal contradiction; the church's refusal to accept our nature as homosexual persons is in conflict with both its central doctrine of incarnation, which requires a sexual-spiritual union, and with the authority of the Melchizedek priesthood which commands a blessing of all life. It is therefore important for every Holy Union to state clearly that what we as a community are doing is acknowledging that God the Creator, the same God presented in the Jewish and Christian scriptures, receives and thereby blesses the union. This proclamation is a bold one which often scandalizes the church. It is my faith that the scandal is inverted and will ultimately restore and heal the church. Our actions can embody a return to the essence of the Gospel, the Good News. Let us look briefly at what a Holy Union looks like while attempting to distinguish it from the social model of marriage.

Two persons, after having completed a year or more living together (a customary requirement), three separate counseling sessions, and a group workshop on relationships, can create an event which symbolizes the union between them. The core act of the Holy Union is the Rite of Blessing, which involves the invocation of God's presence by the spiritual leader of the community. This act is preceded by the mutual exchange of vows and, often, an exchange of rings. The vows of a couple should express the nature of their history and their agreement; the entire ceremony must in some way give voice to what is intended by the couple. I believe that the event should begin with the proclamation of our intention to acknowledge God's blessing and some instruction as to the nature and meaning of blessing. This statement of purpose, along with the vows and blessing, are all that is essential to complete the act. Often, however, a couple will elect to add music and community song as well as the sacrament of Holy Communion.

The addition of these components tends to tie in the more traditional marriage customs. This is proper to the extent that we employ those symbols which express both our uniqueness and intention along with the symbols which have historically communicated bonding and blessing. A Holy Union is a religious ceremony and a spiritual event for people of faith; it is not a reproduction of an American social custom. Hence, gay couples should participate in Holy Unions for spiritual and religious reasons. Those who are not people of faith should not be getting married in churches or synagogues; Holy Unions are for those who have embraced God in their lives. It is not the role of the religious institution to function on behalf of the state in the legalization of anyone's union. That is a business transaction which should be kept separate, relegated to the attorney's and county clerks' offices.

The forum chosen to symbolize the union of two lives should express those two lives; the symbols used need to communicate the nature of the couple's agreement. This means, of course, that each couple's Holy Union will be different since each will have a unique content to their agreement. No two couples will define their union in the same manner; nor should anyone else demand that every pair bonding be a carbon copy of any other. And yet, there will be some commonality to those shared symbols such as the nearly universal exchange of rings and vows, or the offering of a blessing prayer, which have served aptly to affirm and celebrate our relationships.

What do we offer those who do not share a religious faith? I can only suggest that they search for symbols of their own and celebrations which reflect the realities of their own special coupling. These celebrations need not depend upon the religious institutions of our society. There is undoubtedly more integrity in a non-religious approach to celebration for these individuals than if they were to fulfill social dictates and seek a church or synagogue "wedding." What use are religious symbols to affirm and celebrate the relationships of persons who do not profess a religious faith?

This raises again the question of legality. It is important for lesbians and gay men to use the legal instruments available to us to protect property and personal rights. Vastly underused are the instruments of wills and powers of attorney. These should be used by all of us to avoid needless grief and confusion during times of crisis and pain. These legal instruments can answer many questions but, as yet, they do not adequately address all issues; income tax advantages offered to heterosexually married couples, for example, are still unavailable to us.

As for Holy Unions and Rites of Blessing, these are entirely separate from the legal questions affecting any relationship. Even if society were to grant legal sanctions to gay relationships, it is important to keep the Rite of Holy Union separate from the legal issues. The church or synagogue does not need to function on behalf of the state.

As we, lesbian and gay couples, approach the question of how best to celebrate and symbolize our relationships, we need to understand the religious and social dimensions of our choices. Indeed, our decisions have far-reaching political ramifications as we choose to celebrate our unions through a Rite of Blessing or a Holy Union — a choice that will inevitably result in a continuing confrontation with the religious institutions of our society. This choice chips away at the separation between sexuality and spirituality. Every Holy Union, every Rite of Blessing, is both a transformation of ancient symbol and a witness of hope for all people. The Holy Union can be the instrument for symbolizing the union of sexuality and spirituality. Achieving this task is a liberating effort affecting all people.

Does life change? In a sense, when two people celebrate a Holy Union or a Rite of Blessing, they are only giving public expression to a relationship that already exists. The Union is not a magical potion; it does not transform a relationship into something it is not. Often, people will address the subject of a Holy Union as though it were some universal panacea, an insurance policy to guarantee a life together and mutual possession of one another. That is not the purpose of the celebration; while we can certainly give of ourselves to another, no individual is capable of possessing the other.

There is, however, one important change recognized in the Holy Union process. Once two people have shared their witness of love and voiced their covenant before their own community of support and in the presence of God who receives their union, the couple can never again be separated from the effects of that act. They have publicly contracted and there is a reinforcing influence in the community's perception of the couple and, indeed, in the couple's own perception of itself. Even in the event of a separation or dissolution of the union, the parties must return to the original agreement in order to modify or void it.

What happens through the wonder of a Holy Union is that a new entity is being commemorated, and this entity is the "we" of the relationship. The two do not become one but have become a third entity. This change shall never elude the participants. Memories and realities of previous relationships are always part of any relationship. For those reasons, we must state again, deliberate care and thought should precede any choice of a Holy Union.

7

Success

What the Press Won't Print

"Success" means to achieve our goals and, as the term is applied to relationships, it requires a healthy self-esteem. Far too many of us have an incredibly low expectation level for our lives and, consequently, for our relationships. Repeatedly I am asked if I believe gay people can have a successful relationship — the term "success" usually meaning a long-term, even lifetime, union together. Our community's skepticism about the likelihood of long-term gay relationships is founded in part on myth and in part on history. The dramatic rise in the heterosexual divorce rate does not strengthen one's hopes for success in any relationship; gay relationships are further complicated by the lack of adequate role models in our community. Too few of us can point to truly successful gay relationships among our circles of friends. Our low expectations are also influenced by the myth that gay relationships do not last.

Let's address that myth for a moment. Historically, the gay bar has been the social and political center of gay subculture in America. Today, there are hundreds of local and national organizations addressing every facet of our lives as lesbians and gay men, but for decades prior to the explosive growth of the gay rights movement in the United States (dated from the Stonewall Riots of 1969 in New York City), the gay bar was the only major center for community life.

In general, gay bars attract a young, single crowd; there may be a scant handful attracting an older generation, but the primary accent is still upon "single." Gay people in bonded relationships just don't frequent these bars. Behind the scenes, therefore, are literally hundreds of thousands of couples living rather routine daily lives. They work, socialize, attend church, participate in the political process and are engaged in life endeavors not unlike other couples in America. There may be children from a previous heterosexual marriage or by adoption.

These lives are not extraordinary; they are conspicuous only by their absence from the "gay scene." These couples don't count in the dismal statistics of failed gay relationships and yet they represent a vast reality of lifestyle which the press won't cover. The lives of these couples are not newsworthy since they don't fit the exaggerated stereotypes of gay behavior. The current stereotype would have us all in somewhat desperate straits, lonely, and immersed in the constant pursuit of adventuresome sexual escapades. These stories make good copy; the successful relationship outlined in this book is so average in its style and values that it hardly makes the news. Gay couples in America are often the people next door. We are not generally aware of this reality because we have been taught to expect only the stereotypes. Further, our combined lack of relationship skills may be hindering our ability to make friends with those who do not fit the stereotype and who are therefore among the "hidden" gay world.

The successful gay relationship looks much like the successful non-gay one. Take, for example, the two men who met in a Washington, DC, park in 1949 and have been living together since. They are visible in local politics, business and community affairs. On their thirtieth anniversary, they celebrated a Rite of Blessing to mark their history. This event in their home was attended by neighbors and co-workers, many of whom were not gay. Such occasions are becoming more and more common.

Another couple I know of lived together for fifty-five years until one partner died. Their lives and union were a source of hope and strength to many young people around them.

Nor could I forget the two "little old ladies" in their seventies whom I met in 1981. They had shared some fifty-plus years together as lovers. Each looked all the world like everyone's grandmother. They were a great source of joy.

These and countless other stories of successful

relationships demonstrate that pair bonding among gay people which lasts for years and decades is not at all uncommon.

The vast population of gay couples living together for extended periods of time is perhaps the largest portion of gay America. They are not exceptions. But the press won't print the story of mere ordinary people.

Ordinary People

The case of the ordinary person is important to highlight because for those hidden couples to live out ordinary lives by our current social standards and the values of our culture takes a heroic effort. Much energy is required to achieve a "normal" lifestyle since society seeks to withhold at every level the structures, forums, and symbols essential for the affirmation and celebration of our lives. Whether we are coupled or are single, each of us requires a sense of acceptance and affirmation along with healthy and constructive ways to celebrate our lives.

The restrictions of our society are often felt most forcefully at times of crisis, illness, and death. Gay spouses are routinely denied visiting privileges in hospitals since they are not "family." Perhaps the most powerful restrictions come at the time of death. I have watched families show utter disregard for the grief and concerns of a deceased child's lover; some have literally taken over such sensitive details as funeral arrangements and burial sites, often totally excluding their child's lover of many years from this process, and even from attending the funeral itself. Here, the grief process is severely interrupted as the family seeks to absolve itself of its guilt for years of rejection, all the while continuing to reject those who composed the child's true family. Our true families consist of those persons who love, care, and nurture us; this may and should include blood relatives — but often it does not.

This reality presents a continuing argument for the legalization of gay unions. This would allow a spouse's right to take precedence over a family's rights. The right to bury our own is important; I believe that families who have rejected their children have abdicated this right.

The goal of being ordinary requires a great deal of energy. Often, it results in people denying important components of their lives in order to "fit in" to their jobs, their families, their church and society at large. I believe gay men and women should be able to live their lives in complete openness and honesty. The meaning of life's blessing and the rite of blessing our relationship will mean nothing unless we can bless openly all the life around us. We must never surrender this hope that we can live our lives as ordinary people without the costly waste of human energy to accommodate social expectations.

Gay men and lesbians should be accorded the same rights of custom as heterosexuals. This means that public affection can be displayed on the same level as heterosexual couples display their love for one another. There is pain inflicted every time a gay man or woman feels obliged to refer to their spouse as a roommate or friend so as not to offend the social conventions of others or to avoid placing their jobs in jeopardy.

I do not believe that any job is worth the effort of engaging in a constant denial of self and perpetuation of dishonesty. The energy devoted to this accommodation destroys physical and emotional health and gradually chips away at one's self-esteem. Being ordinary people requires an extraordinary effort and we as gay people must be able to acknowledge this effort within ourselves. To acknowledge this effort is to be aware of the daily stress that can endanger our health and relationships if it goes unaddressed.

The ordinary life should be a healthy life free of undue stress. That gay people must expend greater energy to accomplish traditional goals is a constant drain upon energies which could be directed toward the achievement of other goals badly needed by our society, our communities, and ourselves.

Five Stages of Relationship

The joy of a relationship is discovered only with time. As we live in our coupled unions and pursue our vocations, something wonderful happens to us as couples. We begin to develop our corporate identities. This happens as lives merge into shared goals, property, feelings, hopes, and friends. An extended family may develop to include the relatives and parents of the couple as well as close intimate friends. Does this sound so unusual? Certainly not; the pattern of all human relationships is not so uncommon.

Joy comes in the bonding process and it is helpful to know that this process unfolds in stages. These stages can be viewed as (1) discovery, (2) disappointment, (3) decision, (4) development, and (5) destiny.

Discovery. The discovery stage includes the initial meeting and introduction of the two people. This stage incorporates all of the courting and dating dynamics and customs of our culture. It is the one stage most filled with passion and wonder; this is the stage most often exploited by the Hollywood myth. Here is the phase where so many of us get stuck. It is in the discovery period that infatuation is strong and love not yet defined. While this stage is filled with energy, joy, and excitement, it is also filled with ambiguity and confusion.

Disappointment. Stage two is the point at which many couples decide not to continue the relationship. In this stage, the two people encounter reality. The limits and shortcomings of the other become more focused and for a time these shortcomings dominate the horizon. This is a two-way street as both encounter the other's weaknesses. Here, the conflict usually occurs between the myth of a "shopping list lover" and the real qualities of the person at hand. The temptation is to get rid of the one at hand and go out to find the personification of the myth. It is essential to know that this process will repeat itself again and again if one seeks to discover yet another person better suited to one's specifically tailored wants and desires. Discovery is always followed by disappointment and it sometimes appears easier to leave the relationship than to stay.

Decision. Disappointment always brings both people to the point of decision. At this intersection, each must evaluate their goals, and assumptions. Here, clear communication is required to perceive accurately where the other person is. This is a time to take "inventory" as to what you each have invested in the other. Are your assumptions about the relationship open and shared, or is one or both operating on the basis of assumptions not disclosed to the other? Decision is an essential stage in establishing a long-term commitment. The way you encounter with this decision will set the pattern for how you resolve future conflicts.

Disappointment and decision are recurring cycles in any relationship. We must realize that this is not a sad reality to escape but an inevitable human process which can enrich each person's life as each accepts the other partner with all his or her weaknesses and grants the other the freedom to grow and change.

Development. Development is the term I choose to refer to the often extensive period following the decision to continue the relationship. This is a period of nitty-gritty living, change, and growth. It is often characterized by higher levels of security and the growth of trust between two people. The choice to stay carries with it a mutual acknowledgment of each other as persons of worth, persons who are loved. This is a fertile time of commitment which often begins to focus upon the question of a Holy Union, a blessing, and long-range planning such as the mutual purchase of property and the adoption or bearing of children. During this time the pair-bonding agreement is formed in its first structures and old conceptions are often replaced with new mutually-shared ones.

The development stage of the relationship is often the time when the couple begins to publicly acknowledge their pair-bonding to friends, co-workers and families. The time between the discovery and the development stage of a relationship is about six months to one year; I do not think the development stage ever really begins before the sixth month. Understanding that this is a natural process which takes time to develop will ease pressure.

Destiny. The final stage — which may follow a series of decision stages — I am calling "destiny." One dictionary definition of this term is "the predetermined, usually inevitable or irresistible course of events." This is the expression of confidence and assurance that comes with solid and clear agreements. This is the stage of mutual trust and honesty. At this point in a relationship there will be regular and clear communication, a developing ability to face conflict and resolve it, an absence of jealousy and possessiveness, and a mutual independence and freedom. This is a stage of "good health" which allows the future to be a blessing and challenge to be faced together.

This stage of a relationship does not occur until after an extensive period, usually not until the third year or later.

A major problem in gay relationships is our impatient desire to hurry the process along. We cannot leapfrog any stage nor even greatly shorten it. Each must be allowed to unfold naturally. Sometimes, however, the process can be enhanced; this occurs when two people begin the process at the discovery stage with maturity, respect and high levels of trust. This often results from the successful resolution and completion of former relationships. The resolution of previous pair bonding is imperative for the success of our present relationship. A hopeful word here is that one's present relationship, when based on honesty, greatly helps heal the pain and hurt carried over from a previous relationship.

Destiny is the ability and intention to spend a life together in a relationship bonded through time, testing, trust, and honesty. I believe that the symbolization and celebration of a relationship through the Rite of Holy Union should occur only after a couple has reached this stage in its development.

The passage of time proclaims the stable relationships of the ordinary people we have discussed. These are couples whose lives can be models of success for young gay men and women growing up in America. Success means not giving in to the "do your own thing" motto so prevalent in our society; rather success comes with the use of relationship skills and healthy human covenants which allow people to live in community. What may actually occur is that gay men and lesbians will be forced to create models to affirm, symbolize and celebrate our relationships in a social context that does not currently offer support for us. We will thus succeed in reforming our society's model of living in union and may, in so doing, offer the best hope for all relationships. Because of the negative environment in which we must live, we have to give our very best efforts to the task and the product may be our saving the relationships of our non-gay brothers and sisters as we give them this model of wholeness.

Here again, we must boldly affirm and claim the prophetic role of our people and our community. We can offer a healing transformation of the oppressive sex roles which have debilitated American men and women for generations. This is not to suggest that non-gay people do not know success in their relationships, only that we offer symbols of hope badly needed by men and women trapped by rules defined by others.

The freedom to express the depths of human sexuality is crucial in defining all our human relationships. Our essential task is to unify spirituality and sexuality, and to embody this union in our lives and relationships: this is the hinge of hope upon which swings the future of both relationships and family life in America. To avoid the issue of sexual-spiritual wholeness is to forever obstruct the achievement of healthy lives and families in our culture. Homosexuality is not destroying the American family: rather, the issue of homosexuality, when placed in the context of the larger set of all human sexuality and addressed honestly in concert with our spiritual and religious resources, can save the family. This is Good News.

8

The single choice

The Marriage Bias

"When are you going to get married?" "When are you going to settle down?" These questions are frequently addressed to young people by parents and relatives. Starting at the age of sixteen or seventeen, young men and women are besieged with questions about the people they are dating. If a person reaches twenty-five and is still unmarried, the social pressures build. Our culture assumes that everyone is heterosexual and that they should therefore be married and have children; it is "the thing to do."

This bias is almost universal in our culture and it goes unexamined, thus generating a steady pressure on young people to conform to the norm or explain their eccentricities. Moral and ethical arguments are used to reinforce this pressure. What lies beneath the pressure? Why the strong pro-marriage bias? I think there is an underlying fear that unbridled sexual energy will be misused if a person does not get married. We recognize the volatile nature of sexuality and feel compelled to use marriage to control it.

A further reason for our fear about unventilated sexuality is that we have no stated ethics about sex. What we do have are ethics regarding procreation — but not in respect to sex itself. We believe that marriage and sex both revolve around procreation. This entirely leaves out all categories of relationships that do not have procreation as their primary focus. For instance, we teach children the story of creation from Chapter One of Genesis and emphasize that it sets forth the foundation of marriage for the purpose of procreation. At the same time, we ignore the second chapter of Genesis which actually pre-dates the first and focuses upon companionship as the purpose of our bonding. The lack of any sexual ethics which directly and specifically addresses sex in any other context hinders our understanding of the complete role of sex in relationships and gives an unbalanced view of marriage which does not fit the reality of our modern lives. This marriage bias desperately needs re-examination. This biased and pressured environment has caused young gays to view marriage as the only option — particularly among persons who have not "come out" to themselves openly as gay people. Millions of gay people have married because of society's pressures and have raised children, only to discover that this created miserable and unfulfilled lives. Great pain is caused, for themselves and for others, as these men and women claim their identity and choose to live in freedom.

Because the marriage bias has been largely unexamined and unchallenged, people often fall into heterosexual marriages with little or no thought and without the religious counseling we have discussed in earlier chapters. This is a serious mistake for all involved in these "sham" marriages; it is equally damaging for a gay couple who, confident in their sexuality, have nonetheless rushed into a Holy Union for similar unexamined reasons. If couples are asked to live together for at least a year before entering into a Holy Union, why not request this same standard for heterosexual couples? The cry against this unorthodox suggestion is again probably rooted in our fear of sexuality and our confused ethic of procreation as the intended goal of our sexuality. Procreation is the only issue we wish to focus on when the question of sex and relationship arises; yet the dynamics of any relationship far exceed the narrow limits of sexuality and procreation.

Procreation ethics are even more clearly inappropriate in defining gay sex and relationships. We need a new set of ethics. Since a new set of ethics is required for gay and lesbian relationships, why not revolutionize all ethics of sexuality, which appear bankrupt and abnormally off-balance in light of the inappropriateness of a single-minded justification of sex for procreation?

The Ethics of Cruising

Cruising is the process of seeking to meet another person to relate to and with. All single people are engaged in some form of cruising. It is often centered on the exchange of sex — but it need not be. Whether one is walking the street looking for sex or hoping to meet a future date or spouse at a church social, one is cruising. In high school, I used to go out with friends cruising in cars to whistle at girls or pick them up; we were, of course, cruising. Today, young singles frequent bars designed for them to meet and make social contacts. The issue is this: what is a single person to do for relationships, companionship and sexual fulfillment in the face of our society's marriage bias?

First, we must acknowledge the separation of sexuality from procreation. In a world of advanced technology, it is now possible to have sex without babies and babies without sex; therefore, we need to establish some rules by which all people, whether heterosexual or gay, can make sexual choices.

Second, we should consider the following questions as a means of discovering whether a relationship with another person represents a positive and healthy choice or a negative and unhealthy one. These questions should be asked by both people in every relationship:

• Does the relationship fulfill my needs as a person?
• Does the relationship enhance my sense of self-worth?

- Do I feel joy from this relationship?
- Am I more healthy because of this experience?
- Do components of the relationship (including the sexual elements) enhance the dignity of each person?
- Is it mutual, without force or coercion?
- Do I have these same concerns for the other person?

Both people must address these questions to arrive at their individual choice. This process is not necessarily a verbal one but must become a conscious checklist to allow a healthy choice. Relationships which use and abuse the partner or oneself do not possess moral value.

Many times, I have watched gay people express a negative self-image through their sexual and relationship behavior. This tendency to act out a negative self-image in an abusive sexual context occurs far too often in our community and needs to be addressed directly. It often results from internalization of the oppression heaped upon gay people by a culture that will not receive them (i.e., bless them) and seeks to withhold the instruments of affirmation, symbolization and celebration. Our sexual ethic must allow for a healthy affirmation of our selfhood as well as an appropriate symbolization of our meaning as individuals and, when appropriate, as pair-bonded couples.

The single person, by using these guidelines to make choices about sexual partners and activity, can achieve a responsible method of living more fully without incorporating the guilt produced by the traditional reproduction-oriented guidelines.

Sex is a joy as well as an intimate form of communication, love and mutual exchange of power. We must encourage sexual expression that is healthy, responsible, and free of inappropriate procreative restrictions that do not fit the reality of gay and lesbian relationships — and which have not proven effective for heterosexual couples either. Our moral and ethical systems must be based upon choices that produce better health for all. We must come from a positive motivation to *enhance* our lives, rather than to restrict them.

To achieve this human wholeness, we must define what produces health of body, mind and spirit. Each of us, after thinking about the questions above, may come to different conclusions. One person may answer all questions the same as another, yet ultimately make a different choice. What is good and moral for me may not be for you. Our task is to teach people the process of asking questions rather than attempting to teach certain conclusions. We must trust the conclusions a person reaches as right for them, and accept them for their choices.

Making It Alone

The issue of remaining single is still a difficult one. This book assumes a preference for pair-bonding in the gay community, for it appears to me that pair-bonding is a universal process, found in all cultures. In this book, therefore, I try to give pair-bonding in our community a healthy structure. Yet countless people have chosen to live alone, to make no covenant with another. We as a society and we as a gay subculture cannot assume these single people to be unhappy. Those who are unhappy are often so because of constant pressure to be coupled. No doubt this book will add to that bias; yet a single lifestyle can certainly function in moral and healthy ways to include sexual expression. To refrain from making this affirmation is to refuse to accept single people, and to transgress our own cherished task to bless life in all its forms.

Making it alone does not need to be a solitary task, for no one really makes it alone. We are each called to mutual support of one another. The extended family model, wherein couples and singles can live in a mutually supportive environment, is the key here. This model is even more effective when the following universal principle is understood and applied: all persons are gifted by God their Creator with spiritual gifts that enable them to be whole, happy, and healthy, and which in turn enable the larger community to be whole, happy, and healthy.

The interplay among people, single and coupled, heterosexual and gay, male and female, centers around these spiritual gifts. We need to restructure our social fabric to allow a freer interplay among people. Our ethics of relationship, and our imperative to bless life, ultimately create a new commonwealth of people. These people are called to receive one another as gifted, to unite sexuality and spirituality, to enable pair-bonding of all who choose that course regardless of sexual orientation, and to bar no one from the commonwealth.

The point of our prophetic mission as gay and lesbian people is that we are the ones to address this task. Indeed, we have challenged our society on issues of sexuality. Our direction leads inexorably to a commonwealth of all peoples.

The questions surrounding single people in our culture leads us to question our mutuality and interdependence: a sexual ethic for single people leads us to an ethic for all people. The ethical questions for a single person's choice are the same as those that must be asked by two persons in any relationship. The only added consideration in a pair relationship is that decisions must be made by mutual agreement.

Many people would like a set of rules on which to base their choices rather than constantly having to make subjective decisions. But life, when lived to its fullest, requires a constant evaluation in response to an ever-changing world. Rigid rules to govern all of life would prevent us from receiving the unique challenge of every moment. We would, thereby, neglect the blessing of life itself.

9

Prognosis

What the Future Holds

A prognosis is a forecast as to what the future holds. What is the prognosis for gay and lesbian relationships in the future?

Both my own experience with couples and recent studies about gay relationships show a growing number of stable relationships becoming more visible in society at large. Already, current books on social etiquette discuss the appropriate behavior for including gay couples and singles at social gatherings and other social contexts.

The American public must prepare itself for the increasingly more conscious experience of being in *mixed* company. It will become routine in social, business, and political circles to have a person of the same sex introduced as someone's lover or spouse. The future will see the media, especially the visual media, giving a place to gay couples — not as a special feature or as a sensational element of the story line, but rather as another set of normal characters in the drama. This is as it should be.

Middle-class suburban heterosexual couples will find gay and lesbian couples as their neighbors. The days are not far off when traditional mainline churches will find that their pastor is a lesbian with a spouse and children or a gay man who is single or coupled.

In recent years, I have known gay parents whose children are now in elementary school. These children are aware that they are being raised by daddy and his lover or mommie and her best friend. With typical childlike honesty, they share this news with their playmates and schoolmates, and thus non-gay parents may discover their children know much more about gay people than they do. These children will have learned from their friends and may already be accepting the presence of gay couples as normal. This is a source of hope for the future.

The opening of closets and the freedom which attends this event even now reveals teenagers who are fully aware of their sexual orientation as homosexuals. These young gays are refusing to hide who they are. In previously unsupportive environments such as parochial schools and military families, these children are now standing up for their rights; they are affirming their sexual identities as a positive force in their lives.

The blessing of homosexual relationships will

occur outside the current realm of gay religious institutions, as mainline church leaders begin to wrestle
with and resolve the issue of our vocation to bless life.
I know of clergy within the United Methodist, Episco-
pal and Unitarian churches as well as Jewish rabbis
who now perform Rites of Blessing and Holy Unions
for gay and lesbian couples. This is a reality that goes
unnoticed and exists beneath the surface of our American religious community.

Further, the reality that homosexual people pastor congregations in every major denomination in
America is becoming more and more visible. The
graduate schools of theology in America are populated
with gay men and women to a greater percentage than
found in the general population. Seminaries frequently have gay caucuses within them and even
make the issues of gay ministry a part of both curricu-
lum and practical study, offering field experience for
credit to students working in the gay community.
Gay clergy are invited to speak at worship services,
and sexuality has become as important as Biblical
studies. All of this indicates the movement of sexuality and spirituality back together again. The church
faces a new era signifying an end to the sexual-
spiritual split. As this era begins, the changes precipitated may be viewed as radical at first. Nonetheless,
the prognosis is good and the result is healthy — the
future hopeful. Theologies of every school should
herald this age as redemptive and long overdue.

The bottom line for any consideration of the nature of gay relationships or lifestyles is simply that the

future is wide open to us. There is no turning back from the challenge to be free.

Tear Down the Walls

In the years ahead, we will see the rights of gay people discussed and advocated in every political forum in the United States. No place shall be exempt from our movement toward full participation in the life of our society. As we forge new symbols to affirm and celebrate our lives, we shall topple old symbols that no longer serve anyone. The walls which now separate people will crumble as we begin to embrace the realities of the lives around us.

The breaking down of social and cultural distinctions will bring with it a new American vocabulary for relationships, a broader basis of political power, a reformed ethic of sexuality, and a new theology of sexual-spiritual unity. It will transform social structures at every level to accommodate the full participation of gay people.

The doors of the future are open to us as we begin to identify and offer our spiritual gifts to the larger community. I am convinced that the focus from which this future will flow is the act of blessing the Holy Union of two homosexual people. It is this act which confronts and ultimately alters the central images of our culture, our religious systems, and our social practices. The seemingly remote and insignificant act of blessing a Holy Union has within it the power to challenge and restructure our social order. This is because we are redefining the core symbol

upon which Western culture has been built: the nuclear family unit. All the structures that now rest on
the basic family unit must change, shift or fall. This
reality is often feared by religious conservatives as the
major threat to the American family. They are wrong.
Wrong, because the traditional American family unit
must be remodeled if it is to succeed. The present reality is that the nuclear family no longer serves as a
viable model.

Western culture and religions have forced people into
roles which were designed not to free a person's spirit,
but to contain it. We fear sex — we fear its expression,
its violence, and its awesome power. We have sought
to bind our sexuality in the form of legal contracts but
have succeeded only in alienating people from both
the legal and moral sanctions formerly offered by such
contracts. Gay men and women are offering renova-
tion, reformation and new life to old forms. To accept
this revolution is to allow for a new social order and a
new family.

   The new family is profoundly more Biblical than
the nuclear family with which we are so familiar. We
must understand this — even in an age of religious
zealots who seek to make the nuclear family of America synonymous with God's Plan for Creation. The
new family I refer to is more akin to the one defined
by Jesus in Matthew 12, Mark 3, and Luke 9. The
disciples came to Jesus to tell him that his mother and
brother were waiting for him. His reply was, "who is
my mother, who is my brother, but he who does the

will of God is my mother, my brother, my sister."

Here is a radical restructuring of the family unit — from the Bible. We are not bound by blood or marriage but by the spirit of love and acceptance. Therefore, our allegiance to those who love and accept us constitutes the basic framework for our *real* family. This message must be heard by every child who has been rejected by family, and by every parent who has been rejected by a child. This is hope for gay people — hope which comes in the words of Jesus, the one who is called a priest after the order of Melchizedek, the one who has changed the law.

Modern religious zealots seeking to condemn gay people are missing the fundamental revelation implicit in the structuring of our relationships. Rather than a threat, this realignment of the central symbols of our culture is necessary for the survival of all our relationships as well as the fulfillment of both our religious and political creeds. Our religious creeds demand love and acceptance of all people, while our political creeds demand justice and equality for all people. This transformation of the central cultural symbols shall therefore guarantee our faithfulness to these creeds.

What I have stated here is not a utopian vision but rather a reasonable expectation of what will happen within the remaining years of the twentieth century. If anything, this forecast is conservative, as it is based upon the extension of current and visible trends and does not incorporate at all or suppose any radical or revolutionary social realignment. My forecasts are based upon a reasonable examination of current social, political and theological trends.

Are We Willing To Succeed?

The face of the future and the achievement of this prognosis rests solely upon the will of each gay man and woman in America. Success is a product of our willingness to risk.

As we *discover* what the future can bring, this discovery breeds excitement, passion, and hope. But, much like our relationship behavior, our political ventures are fraught with myths that ignore the realities of life. So, therefore, we may ultimately encounter *disappointment* and we are prone to quit, to believe that the risk is too great, the rewards not worth it, or the goal unachievable. We are often likely to give up, to go back to our more comfortable ways of behavior, even though this signals a return to oppression and bondage.

Disappointment leads to *decision:* shall we fight or give up? Giving up means waiting again for the discovery of a new hope, but it also means that our ability to grasp any new hope is seriously impaired.

Going on leads us into the fertile fields of *development.* Many gay and lesbian organizations in America today are presently reaping the benefits of the developmental stage. We are building new structures for the future and embracing subgroups of gay people who have previously been left out. Many of our brothers and sisters are themselves in the developmental stage. They must be touched by the energy and promise of our organizations if they are to move into the hope of the forecast I have projected. To so touch them, we must create an environment that will allow each of them to choose to move out of the closets of fear and hiding.

The final stage of *destiny* is the achievement of the vision of our future. Again, I must affirm that portions of this vision are being presently fulfilled in the lives of some of us. The dream is not a far-off illusion but a timeless reality to be grasped now.

Our willingness to succeed — to discover the vision — rests upon our willingness to come out of hiding. I believe we must each arrive at certain conclusions if we are to participate significantly in the future with joy and wholeness.

- Dishonesty is always too high a price to be paid to maintain any relationship.
- Dishonesty and its compromise of integrity and selfhood will make me emotionally, mentally and physically sick.
- No family expectation is worth my compromise of who I am.
- No economic system can own my life or dictate my behavior; I can't be bought at any price.
- My true family members are those who support, nurture and love me.
- My purpose in life is to be fully able and willing to offer my spiritual gifts so that my community and I can be healthy and blessed.
- My faith assures me that all my life's true needs will be met.

- My personal prosperity is found in my learning to give of myself and to receive from others.
- I have God-given authority and power to fulfill my life. No one else can give it to me or take it from me.

These conclusions are the product of observation, testing and experience. They represent the essential truths upon which a relationship should rest. The truth is that people must first love themselves in order to form long-lasting and successful relationships. Here is our challenge: self-image and self-esteem will determine the health of our relationships. Very simply put, if I do not love myself, why should I expect another to love me? When people lack self-esteem and self-love, they will communicate this to the world around them. Others will not be drawn to them but will be put off without even a conscious awareness of these dynamics.

Self-esteem is far more important in influencing our ability to form relationships than is physical appearance or sexual prowess. This is a discovery we all need to make.

Therefore, the key to the future — to the fulfillment of the vision of our community and of our personal goals — rests in ourselves, and in liberation of ourselves.

One liberated, self-assured, healthy person can change the world. As you become that person, the world will beat a path to your door. The real questions are these: Are we willing to accept freedom? Are we willing to risk, to choose, to succeed? Experience confirms that many people would rather stay in the comfort of the present reality which they know — no matter how negative — than risk and venture out.

Incorporating these conclusions in our lives is not simple or easy; but it is the only alternative we have. The choice before us is life or death. We must choose life — if only for the sake of the gay men and lesbians who before us chose death. When we choose life, we build upon the positive choices of others before us; we also create the possibilities for life for those who shall follow us.

10
Afterword

My own personal journal as a gay man has provided the basis for this book. My own pattern of life has followed the stages of development I have described in this book.

Discovery: I discovered my own sexual identity at a very early age. I knew that I always had been attracted to men. The discovery was exciting and frightening and has led me to a fulfilling relationship, a satisfying vocation and unquenchable hope for my life and the lives of all gay people. The discovery goes on.

Disappointment: Woven throughout every part of my experience, disappointment threatened to undo me. I was disappointed that my religious training omitted my sexuality or any sexuality. Relationships around me, all of my role models, disappointed me. The standards and symbols offered me never seemed to affirm my life or touch the deeper knowledge within me. My first relationship lasted seven years and offered me constant disappointment. This pattern and presence of disillusionment in life was dragging me down into deep depression and almost annihilated my self-image.

Nowhere could I find affirmation of life or relationship. There was nothing to celebrate. I am sure that many gay people today are stuck at this level of development.

Disappointment and disillusionment led me to the *decision* stage. I saw many people attempt to fit their lives into the expectations of others. They sometimes destroyed their lives in the process. Some just didn't bother trying to fit. They decided to end their lives.

My decision was the opposite: There had to be something more. My life and sexual identity were not a mistake. It had to have some purpose. If my faith meant anything, it had to mean that God wanted me to use what I was as a way to free others and make my life work. So I decided to claim all the promises of my faith; I decided to affirm my sexuality as a gift from God. I decided that life would be joyful and wonderful and I decided that God would never forget my needs — even my sexual ones — so I need not worry. I laid down my grief, guilt, and regret. I decided to live life in its abundance. This was part of the promise I claimed. It was my point of decision and it changed my life.

Development was next and it was a joy too. The development was simple: life started working; I liked myself and I knew life was good. All the memories and pain of disillusionment faded away because I met a man named Alan B. Fox who embodied the symbols of affirmation and celebration. He was, and still is at present, my Melchizedek. His response to me was to embrace and accept all that I was. This excited me to begin to accept and to experience healing of the past pain and disappointment.

The development stage of my life did not begin until I was thirty-two years old — this is an important note for every young reader who is worried about not having life together before twenty-five. Development meant time to grow in love and relationship; time to express the unity of my sexuality and my spirituality. Development meant grasping the future to change it and fill it with my gifts. This stage has been a time to replace all the old patterns of negative ideas and destructive lifestyle with a positive affirmation of my life, my love and my community. The relationship with Alan reveals the symbols of celebration as we together discover Holy Union. What develops is gratitude and power to live. We learn together how to give to ourselves, to each other and to the world. Now, this is *Destiny*.

Destiny is all of our tomorrows. Surely, there will always be a pattern of discovery, disappointment and decision through all our lives but we can now embrace the pattern with hope and with a confident acceptance. The priesthood of Melchizedek means that there is no part of life we cannot receive, or, to put it in another way, there is nothing we cannot handle.

Destiny now means that we shall transform the world, for the power we possess is the greatest power on earth — the power of actualized selfhood; the power of giving of spiritual gifts; the power of spirit merged in the flesh. An idea embodied in human flesh is all the world needs for life in abundance.

I am convinced that when a person is captured by truth, they can do whatever they choose as long as they never compromise that essential truth. Oppression for gay people ends at the moment we no longer choose to participate in it.

The substance of our symbols, our ability to affirm, and our will to celebrate the "two of us" and "all of us," as gay people, lives within us.

Appendix

A. Contract of Commitment — Romantic Version

This "contract," drafted by a lawyer with a lawyer's touch for form and that incomprehensible language so favored by attorneys, was described by a colleague of mine as an "attorney's love letter." Thus, since it really expresses the basis for a depth of a commitment — rather than dealing with those areas of daily life together that may give rise to dispute, I have characterized it here as the "romantic version" of a commitment between spouses.

Contract of Commitment

This contract, made and entered into this 24th day of June, 1982, by and between D, an individual citizen and resident of Bethesda, Maryland; and B, also an individual citizen and resident of Bethesda, Maryland:

WITNESSETH:

WHEREAS, on or about the 28th day of August, 1981, under the auspices of the Metropolitan Community Church of Washington, DC, D and B were mysteriously and inexplicably drawn together by virtual accident of fate; and

WHEREAS, thereafter on or about the 25th day of September, 1981, D and B furthered the extent and nature of their relationship under the guise of an abortive "date" and therein began the nurturing process of developing both love and desire for one another; and

WHEREAS, on or about the 10th day of October, on the occasion of the celebration of B, the parties discovered the sheer joy of spending time in the company of one another; and

WHEREAS, on or about the 13th day of October, 1981, the parties resolves — albeit then on tentatively — to dedicate substantial energy toward the relationship then discovered to be so promising between them, sealing that resolution with a mutual recognition of "how good they would be together"; and

WHEREAS, from time to time thereafter and no later than Friday, November 27, 1981, the parties began to consider in earnest the prospects for spending their lives together; and

WHEREAS, during the months of December 1981 and January 1982, they began to establish a joint and mutual household under an implicit, as well as an express, assumption that such household would continue uninterrupted for the rest of their lives; and

WHEREAS, on April 2, 1982, the relationship of B and D was blessed, by God, by them and by their friends, in a Rite of Blessing conducted at the Metropolitan Community Church of Washington, DC, testifying to each other and in the presence of God and their friends to the extent of their love and commitment; and

WHEREAS, the parties now desire that this commitment be formalized in a manner which is legally binding as well as spiritually fulfilling; which is not only enforceable at law and in equity but in the eyes of each other and in the eyes of God, having the full force and effect of a contract of marriage;

NOW, THEREFORE, in consideration of the mutual covenants and promises herein contained, the parties do hereby agree and commit as follows;

1. Commitment. By this instrument, D and B hereby irrevocably commit their respective lives to the other, as more explicitly defined in this Contract.

2. Duration of Commitment. Such commitment shall remain in force for the remainder of their natural lives and, God willing, through eternity and beyond, all without exception.

3. Extent of Commitment. Such commitment shall be, in all respects, total and consuming. Without intending limitation hereby, the commitment shall include every condition and element of the state of legally sanctioned matrimony, acknowledging that the matrimony intended by the Contract is indeed sanctioned in the hearts of the participants, by God, and by those who truly love and care for B and D. Such commitment shall include, merely by way of example, total financial dedication one to the other, including full and complete disclosure of all financial matters and absolute and unfettered sharing of all assets and liabilities between them. Further, such commitment shall include unlimited care and concern for every facet of the life of the other; abiding interest in the education, development and career of the other; delicate care and treatment when the other is mentally or physically debilitated — for even the slightest perceived ailment or disability, mental or physical; adoption of and love for the other's family; sharing of every thought and feeling without reservation or fear, holding nothing from the other; spending every waking and sleeping moment together possible for the rest of their lives; laughing, crying, hugging, holding, making incredible passionate love, touching, comforting, relaxing, soothing away tensions, taking care of the most mundane household details for the other; expecting nothing but the best from the other but harboring neither disappointment nor resentment when the other may fall short of that expectation; and, most importantly, dedicating every fiber of their beings toward assuring the continuity and perpetuity of the magical quality of their relationship, forever and ever.

4. Conditions of Commitment. Without even inconsequential exception, the commitment of B and D one to the other hereunder shall be unconditional and unqualified, irrespective of changes in circumstances, states of health and well-being, and external factors of every kind and description. Such commitment made today is total and absolute, reserving nothing.

5. Enforceability of Commitment. It is the full intent of the parties that this Contract of Commitment shall be legally binding in all respects, enforceable in any court of law or equity having jurisdiction of the parties and that this Contract shall be the equivalent of a contract of marriage, solemnized at law and in religion. And, while it is the intent of the parties that the Contract of Commitment shall be formalized and publicly proclaimed at an appropriate ceremony to be held in a religious setting in December 1982, neither the tenor of nor the durability of the commitments made in this Contract are dependent upon such public proclamation.

IN WITNESS WHEREOF, the parties have executed this Contract of Commitment effective as of the day and year first above written.

_____
Signature: D

_____
Signature: B

WITNESSED:

_____

_____

B. Contract of Commitment — Legalistic Version

There are as many different forms of contracts as there are couples in this world with a need to contract. Indeed, there is such a variety of topics about which couples need to reach consensus, the following brief outline can only be considered as a sampling of the kinds of subjects a couple might consider. It is, I believe, important first that the subjects be addressed, that some form of rational and workable agreement be reached, and that these agreements be committed to writing. Even if you and your spouse are only able to reach agreement on one or two items (for now), it is wise to record these "agreements" and move on to work out those areas where agreement is more difficult.

Contract of Commitment

On _____, 1983, (A)_____ and (B)_____ fully discussed several important aspects of their living together and want hereby to record the agreements reached. It is recognized that, in reaching these agreements, both parties have made compromises and, it is in the spirit of cooperation and fostering a healthy and mutually beneficial relationship that these agreements are today deemed important.

1. **Financial Agreements.** In recognition of the unequal income status of A and B, monthly rental required for the apartment (or any other residence acquired or shared by A and B) will be paid jointly with A paying 75% of such rental and B paying 25%. All utilities, telephone charges, miscellaneous household items (including cleaning and personal grooming supplies), groceries and all other normal and ordinary

household expenses will be shared by A and B on an equal basis. Personal clothing and other personal items will be paid for by the party purchasing the item. All major household expenditures, including new furnishings, will be subject to independent agreement as to cost-splitting, with the basic understanding that the cost of such items will be shared in direct proportion to the parties' relative ability at the time to absorb such costs. At this time, the parties shall not establish a joint checking or other banking account, with the recognition that such account might at some future date be appropriate.

2. Household Property; Automobiles. In recognition that both parties brought to the household a relatively equal amount of household furnishings and appliances, and have roughly shared on an equal basis in the acquisition cost of such items purchased during the relationship, all such household property shall be considered by A and B to be jointly owned. Disposition of any such item of property will be by mutual agreement only. In recognition of the fact that the personal automobiles of A and B were personally acquired by each without financial assistance from the other, the ownership of each individual's automobile (and the financial responsibility for its upkeep, taxes, licensing and insurance) will remain with the individual and shall not be shared.

3. Basic Household Duties. In recognition of both the parties' respective abilities and available time, A agrees to assume primary responsibility for all cooking, while B shall be primarily responsible for household maintenance and cleaning. All other household chores, including gardening, shoveling snow, mowing the lawn, minor repairs, washing and ironing will be shared on as nearly an equal basis as possible. Errands, including picking up and delivering laundry and dry cleaning, post office visits, grocery shopping, and other miscellaneous household shopping will also be performed jointly and mutually — together when possible; provided, however, that, in recognition of the greater availability of leisure or non-working time to B, B shall assume primary responsibility for performing such errands at times when A is working.

4. Family Obligations. Both parties acknowledge their love and devotion to their respective families. Thus, to the extent that holidays and other occasions for family gatherings pose conflicts, such conflicts shall be resolved as nearly as possible by A and B making family visits or performing other family obligations on a rotating basis. For example, if Christmas one year is spent with the family of A, every effort will be made to spend the following Christmas with the family of B. Both parties acknowledge, however, the importance of, first, being together with one anther on these holidays and family occasions and, second, of sharing their families and their love for those families with one another.

5. Religion. It is recognized that A is not currently actively involved in any organized religion; on the other hand, B is an active member of the Metropolitan Community Church. Both parties here confirm their respect for the positions of the other, recognizing fully the right of B regularly to attend church services and the right of A to refrain from any active practice of religion.

6. Closed Relationship. Having fully considered and discussed the alternatives, it is the decision of A and B at this time to maintain a closed relationship. It is further agreed that this consensus will not be breached by either party without a full and complete prior discussion between them.

7. Amendments. It is finally recognized that this contract is incomplete in that it does not address every potential area for major or minor conflict between A and B. To that extent, it is intended that this contract be subject at all times to amendment, following complete and open discussion and agreement between A and B, which amendment must be reduced to writing and attached to this basic agreement for it to be effective and binding. Both parties also here acknowledge their continued willingness to address areas of future conflict and to exert every reasonable effort to reach agreement on each such subject, with the ultimate goal of reducing each such agreement to writing, as a modification to this contract.

Dated the _____ day of _____, 1983 in Washington, DC

_____

Signature, A

_____

Signature, B

C. Order of Worship — Holy Union

The following order of worship was taken from the program of my own Holy Union with Alan on July 18, 1980:

Prelude
Processional Hymn — *All Creatures of Our God and King*
Invocation
Welcome
Scripture: I John 4:7–19
Act of Praise
Hymn of the Word — *Spirit of the Living God*
Solo
The Rite of Holy Union
   Charge to the Couple
   The Covenant
   The Prayer of the Couple
   Charge to the Community
   The Blessing
Hymn of Preparation — *O God, Our Help in Ages Past*
Holy Communion
Recessional Hymn — *Rejoice, the Lord Is King*
Benediction
Postlude

D. Rite of Holy Union — Simple Format

Welcome and Introduction (explaining the meaning of the blessing)

Prayer (offering the service to God)

Scripture (appropriate selections on love and relationship)

The Rite of Holy Union:

    Charge to the Couple and Congregation (stating our mutual responsibilities)

    Exchange of Vows (in language and symbols which reflect the couple's agreement and contract)

    Blessing of Rings

    Prayer of Blessing (offered by clergy to name and proclaim the sealing of the covenant)

Final Prayer of Benediction

E. Order of Worship — Rite of Blessing

Welcome

Readings — Scriptural and Secular

Support of Witnesses and Friends

Special Music

A Time for Sharing Between the Couple

Prayer of Blessing

Exchange of Peace

Holy Communion (optional)

Lord's Prayer

Benediction